AWARDS

Classics, Gems &
Buried Treasures

DETROIT • WASHINGTON, D.C. • LONDON

EDITORS

Martin Connors

Les Stone

Christine Tomassini

And a Big Hand to:

Shanna Heilveil

Julia Furtaw

Diane L. Dupuis

Beth Fhaner

James Craddock

Don Wellman

Designer
Mary Krzewinski

Typesetter
Marco Di Vita
Graphix Group

Photos courtesy of The Kobal Collection

A Cunning Canine Production
Copyright © 1995 by Visible Ink Press
Published by Visible Ink Press™ a division of
Gale Research Inc., 835 Penobscot Bldg.
Detroit, MI 48226-4094

WHAT'S EATING GILBERT GRAPE
(1993) 118m PG-13
*Leonardo DiCaprio, Juliette Lewis,
Mary Steenburgen*
D: Lasse Hallstrom

Depp heads a strong cast in this tale of an extremely dysfunctional family in small-town Iowa directed by *My Life as a Dog* Hallstrom. Depp, a model of sanity considering his circumstances, works in a grocery store and cares for his mother, an obese woman who hasn't been able to leave home for seven years. He also keeps an eye on his brother (superbly portrayed by DiCaprio), a mentally retarded 17-year-old who constantly wanders away to climb the town watertower. Interesting to see Depp, who specializes in weirdos, playing the normal one for a change. Of course, he followed with *Ed Wood*.

Headliners:

Ed Wood (1994)

Benny and Joon (1993)

Cry-Baby (1990)

Edward Scissorhands (1990)

Good Support:

Platoon (1986)

A Nightmare on Elm Street (1984)

And the nominees are:

Johnny Belinda
(1948) 103m
Jane Wyman, Lew Ayres
D: Jean Negulesco
Deaf single parent tries to keep child despite her father's efforts. Wyman won the Oscar for this one.

Children of a Lesser God
(1986) 119m R
William Hurt, Marlee Matlin
D: Randa Haines
Unorthodox speech teacher at deaf school falls in love with rebellious ex-student. Based on Mark Medoff's play.

The Miracle Worker
(1962) 107m
Anne Bancroft, Patty Duke
D: Arthur Penn
Based on the true story of blind and deaf Helen Keller and how teacher Anne Sullivan taughter her how to communicate with the world. Good '79 remake as well.

One Flew Over the Cuckoo's Nest
(1975) 129m R
Jack Nicholson, Louise Fletcher
D: Milos Forman
Effective adaptation of Ken Kesey's novel, featuring a two-bit crook who decides to feign insanity so he will be sent to a mental hospital rather than prison. This is a big mistake.

Passion Fish
(1992) 136m R
Mary McDonnell, Alfre Woodward
D: John Sayles
Paralyzed, bitter actress becomes charge of live-in nurse already plagued with personal problems. McDonnell moving despite not moving.

Rain Man
(1988) 128m R
Dustin Hoffman, Tom Cruise
D: Barry Levinson
Smarmy young man gains measure of maturity after abducting autistic brother and traveling cross country. Hoffman is excellent as idiot savant, Cruise holds own (no small task) as jerk who becomes caring person.

Scent of a Woman
(1992) 157m R
Al Pacino, Chris O'Donnell
D: Martin Brest
Blind, bitter ex-colonel becomes charge of game youth and takes him for last whirl before committing suicide. Pacino more overpowering than usual but does swell tango with Gabrielle Anwar.

Wait Until Dark
(1967) 107m
Audrey Hepburn, Alan Arkin
D: Terence Young
Blind woman is terrorized by murderous thieves anxious to recover drugs her husband inadvertently smuggled into country. Lights out.

The Waterdance
(1991) 106m R
Eric Stoltz, Wesley Snipes, Helen Hunt
D: Neal Jimenez, Michael Steinberg
Writer, paralyzed in hiking accident, tries to handle rehab, fellow patients, and his married lover. Deals unsentimentally with physical adjustments, including sex.

And the winner is:

My Left Foot

(1989) 103m R

Daniel Day-Lewis, Brenda Fricker

D: Jim Sheridan

Day-Lewis is extraordinary in true story of Christy Brown, a cerebral-palsy sufferer who overcame all-manner of obstacles to become a painter and writer. Fricker's wonderful as his caring ma.

Best Films That Oscar Ignored

Brazil
(1985) 131m R
Jonathan Price, Robert De Niro
D: Terry Gilliam
Hallucinatory, futuristic work in which world seems overwhelmed by heating ducts. De Niro astounds as heroic repairman. Monty Python's Michael Palin acts truly weird performance.

Cutter's Way
(1981) 105m R
Jeff Bridges, John Heard
D: Ivan Passer
Disabled veteran suspects fatcat of mayhem and engages friend in effort to uncover the truth. Unusually cynical mystery from the novel by Newton Thorburg.

Enemies, A Love Story
(1989) 119m R
Ron Silver, Lena Olin
D: Paul Mazursky
Intense, disturbing portrait of Holocaust survivor and his problems with women. Atypically sensitive work from director of often superficial fare.

Fat City
(1972) 93m PG
Stacy Keach, Jeff Bridges
D: John Huston
Alcoholic, over-the-hill boxer attempts comeback. Incredibly enough, he has a protege. Unflinching depiction of violent world.

Heart Like a Wheel
(1983) 113m PG
Bonnie Bedelia, Beau Bridges
D: Jonathan Kaplan
Story of celebrated drag racer Shirley Muldowney. Bedelia delivers one of *the* great film performances.

Henry and June
(1990) 136m NC-17
Fred Ward, Uma Thurman, Maria De Medeiros
D: Philip Kaufman
Intense trio talk about and have sex in '30s Paris. Then they talk about sex some more. Then they have more sex. Then they write about it.

Once Upon a Time in America
(1984) 225m R
Robert De Niro, James Woods
D: Sergio Leone
Loopy saga of boyhood friends who become gangsters. Sort of *The Godfather* meets *The Good, the Bad, and the Ugly*.

Straight Time
(1978) 114m R
Dustin Hoffman, Theresa Russell
D: Ulu Grosbard
Grim, unsettling drama about small-time thief. Hoffman has never been better. Entire supporting cast shines too.

Sweet Smell of Success
(1957) 96m
Burt Lancaster, Tony Curtis
D: Alexander MacKendrick
Grim look at world of scheming gossip columnist and equally worthless hangers-on. What *The Bonfire of the Vanities* wanted to be.

After Hours
(1986) 97m R
Griffin Dunne, Rosanna Arquette
D: Martin Scorsese
Unwholesome, excellent comedy about yuppie who befriends sexy woman and soon finds himself in nightmare world of duplicity and violence.

Platoon
(1987) 113m R
Charlie Sheen, Willem Dafoe, Tom Berenger
D: Oliver Stone
Dull boy finds both good and evil while fighting in Vietnam. Dafoe and Berenger are both impressive.

River's Edge
(1988) 99m R
Keanu Reeves, Dennis Hopper
D: Tim Hunter
Drug-crazed dude chokes girlfriend, conducts friends to her corpse. So what'd you do at school today?

Stand and Deliver
(1989) 105m PG
Edward James Olmos, Lou Diamond Phillips
D: Ramon Menendez
Tough teacher inspires interest in calculus from East L.A. barrio students.

sex, lies and videotape
(1990) 101m R
James Spader, Andie MacDowell
D: Steven Soderberg
Gloomy drifter undoes college friend's life with personal videotapes of friend's wife and lover.

The Grifters
(1991) 114m R
John Cusack, Anjelica Huston, Annette Bening
D: Stephen Frears
Unflinching drama about seedy con artists. Cusack is sympathetic as fellow with both untrustworthy girlfriend and scheming, equally untrustworthy mother.

Rambling Rose
(1992) 115m R
Laura Dern, Robert Duvall
D: Martha Coolidge
Sexually carefree woman exerts powerful hold on various men in Southern household during Depression. Dern impresses in lead, Duvall delivers usual greatness.

The Player
(1993) 123m R
Tim Robbins, Greta Scacchi
D: Robert Altman
Black comedy about soulless Hollywood exec who commits murder and tries to cover his tracks. Film features more than 50 cameos.

Short Cuts
(1993) 189m R
Tim Robbins, Anne Archer
D: Robert Altman
Endlessly entertaining cross-section of L.A. culture features a wide range of characters and situations. Derives, improbably enough, from Raymond Carver's tales.

Best Directorial Debuts by Stars

A Bronx Tale
(1993) 122m R
Chazz Palminteri, Robert De Niro
D: Robert De Niro
Boy with bus driver dad admires local gangster. Sort of like a Scorsese movie. Then again, sort of not.

Dances with Wolves
(1990) 181m PG-13
Kevin Costner, Mary McDonnell
D: Kevin Costner
Civil War veteran finds adventure and spiritual insight on the Indian frontiers. Great buffalo stampede.

Falling from Grace
(1992) 100 PG-13
John Mellencamp, Mariel Hemingway
D: John Mellencamp
Country stud returns to Indiana town for his grandfather's 80th birthday, has an affair with his brother's wife who is also having an affair with the hero's father (her father-in-law). Just a lonely old night.

Hide in Plain Sight
(1980) 96m PG
James Caan, Jill Eikenberry
D: James Caan
Worker searches for children who vanished when his ex-wife and her mobster husband were relocated by government's secret witness program.

Little Man Tate
(1991) 99m PG
Jodie Foster, Dianne Wiest, Adam Hann-Byrd
D: Jodie Foster
Genius tyke is torn between loving mother and domineering school director. Isn't everybody?

The Night of the Hunter
(1955) 93m
Robert Mitchum, Shelley Winters
D: Charles Laughton
Psychotic preacher terrorizes widow and two children, though he's not a televangelist. A truly frightening film anyway.

One-Eyed Jacks
(1961) 141m
Marlon Brando, Karl Malden
D: Marlon Brando
Thief is abandoned by partner. Years later, thief wanders into town. Guess who's the sheriff. Brando is Rio. Malden is Dad. Movie's okay.

Ordinary People
(1980) 124m R
Timothy Hutton, Mary Tyler Moore
D: Robert Redford
Teenager tortures himself over brother's accidental death. His brittle mom's not too understanding.

Rachel, Rachel
(1968) 102m R
Joanne Woodward, James Olson
D: Paul Newman
Sexually repressed spinster schoolteacher gets one last chance at romance. As if Springsteen's *Thunder Road* were sung to Ruth Buzzi.

▶

Dances with Wolves (1990)

And the nominees are:

For a Few Dollars More
(1965) 127m PG
Clint Eastwood, Lee Van Cleef
D: Sergio Leone
Bounty hunter and gunslinger
enter into uneasy pact to track band
of sadistic bandits. Many memorable shootouts.

Fort Apache
(1948) 125m
John Wayne, Henry Fonda
D: John Ford
By-the-book officer decides it's my
way or the highway at western cal-
vary outpost. But the Duke has his
own way of doing things. May not
be PC but it's very mythic American.

High Plains Drifter
(1973) 105m R
Clint Eastwood, Verna Bloom
D: Clint Eastwood
Grueling account of drifter who exacts gruesome revenge on entire
town. "Paint this town red."

My Darling Clementine
(1946) 97m
Henry Fonda, Victor Mature
D: John Ford
Meditative account of gunfight at
the O.K. Corral. Fonda's Earp is fascinating study.

Red River
(1948) 133m
John Wayne, Montgomery Clift
D: Howard Hawks
Father and son conduct battle of

wills on cattle drive. Wayne masterful as obsessed, domineering boss.
Clift equally fine as more sensitive
soul. "Take 'em to the river, Matt."

Rio Bravo
(1959) 140m
John Wayne, Dean Martin
D: Howard Hawks
Tough sheriff in border town awaits
attack from murderous mates of
gunman he's arrested. Chance, Dude,
Colorado, Feathers, and Stumpy,
they're all here. Explosive climax.

The Searchers
(1956) 119m
John Wayne, Jeffrey Hunter
D: John Ford
Hard-hearted frontiersman devotes
years to doggedly tracking niece
kidnapped by Indians. Particularly
moving finale.

Stagecoach
(1939) 100m
John Wayne, Claire Trevor
D: John Ford
Strangers band together when their
coach is besieged by bandits and In-
dians. Wayne fierce as gun-toting
Ringo Kid.

Tombstone
(1993) 130m R
Kurt Russell, Sam Elliott
D: George P. Cosmatos
Giant mustaches dominate screen
as Wyatt and the boys reluctantly
defend the town against despicable

villains. Val Kilmer's spin on tubercular Doc Holliday is a must see.

Unforgiven
(1992) 131m R
Clint Eastwood, Gene Hackman
D: Clint Eastwood
Gunfighter reluctantly ends retire-

ment, runs afoul of sadistic sheriff. Stunning cast, unflinching drama.

And the winner is:

The Man Who Shot Liberty Valance

(1962) 123m

John Wayne, James Stewart, Lee Marvin

D: John Ford

Idealist lawyer and tough cowboy reluctantly join forces to rid town of despicable, bloodthirsty bully. Star trio excel, and final shootout is Zapruder moment of entire genre.

Dead Ringers
(1988) 117m R
Jeremy Irons, Genevieve Bujold
D: David Cronenberg
Irons plays psychotic twin gynecologists in this, one of Cronenberg's tamer efforts. Still, it gets kinda gross.

The Family Jewels
(1965) 100m
Jerry Lewis
D: Jerry Lewis
Insufferable heiress must select a stepfather from among six goofy uncles, played by guess who.

Georgia
(1987) 90m
Judy Davis, John Bach
D: Ben Lewin
Lawyer probes the demise of her freewheeling mother. Versatile Davis is compelling in both parts.

The Hotel New Hampshire
(1984) 110m R
Jodie Foster, Rob Lowe
D: Tony Richardson
Comedy-drama about incredibly weird family has Matthew Modine serving double time as a rapist and a French terrorist. Novel by John Irving.

Jack's Back
(1987) 97m R
James Spader
D: Rowdy Harrington
Spader plays wildly contrasting parts as both sincere doctor to the poor and reckless brother accused of murder.

Kind Hearts and Coronets
(1949) 104m
Alec Guinness, Dennis Price
D: Robert Hamer
Unlikely comedy in which cold-blooded rogue eliminates 8 relatives (all played by Guinness) coming between him and a substantial inheritance.

The Mouse That Roared
(1959) 83m
Peter Sellers, Jean Seberg
D: Jack Arnold
Sellers spreads himself around in this comedy about a country's efforts to lose a war against America and thus qualify for foreign aid.

Start the Revolution Without Me
(1970) 91m PG-13
Donald Sutherland, Gene Wilder
D: Bud Yorkin
Sutherland and Wilder each work double duty in this French Revolution spoof about switched sets of twins.

The Grey Fox
(1983) 92m PG
*Richard Farnsworth, Jackie
    Burroughs*
D: Phillip Borsos
Kindly old stagecoach robber completes 30 years in prison and finds the world changed. Fine vehicle for Farnsworth.

The Terry Fox Story
(1984) 96m
Eric Fryer, Robert Duvall
D: Ralph L. Thomas
Inspirational, true-life tale of cancer survivor who embarks on marathon across Canada despite artificial right leg.

The Bay Boy
(1985) 107m R
Kiefer Sutherland, Liv Ullmann
D: Daniel Petrie
Depression-era drama concerns youth whose adolescent angst intensifies when he witnesses a murder.

My American Cousin
(1986) 94m PG
Margaret Langrick, John Wildman
D: Sandy Wilson
Plucky adolescent girl falls in love with her fetching, 17-year-old American cousin during a summer vacation.

**The Decline of the American
    Empire**
(1987) 102m R
*Dominique Michel, Dorothee
    Berryman*
D: Denys Arcand
Various self-absorbed friends explore their insecurities. You'll want to explore fast forward.

Night Zoo
(1988) 115m
Filles Maheu, Roger Le Bel
D: Jean-Claude Lauzon
Weird account of father-son reconciliation and Montreal's lurid underground of drugs and illicit sex. Vivid, occasionally unnerving.

Jesus of Montreal
(1990) 119m R
Lothaire Bluteau, Gilles Pelletier
D: Denys Arcand
Vagrant actor takes on Passion Play, outrages local clergy. Strong performance from Bluteau.

Naked Lunch
(1992) 117m R
Peter Weller, Judy Davis
D: David Cronenberg
Based on William Burroughs's hallucinatory account of drug-addict writer. Novel's sex is considerably diminished, but much weirdness is retained.

**32 Short Films about Glenn
    Gould**
(1993) 93m
Colm Feore
D: Francois Girard
Fascinating take on life of peculiar pianist who withdrew from touring and devoted himself to recording, traveling in northern Canada, and abusing pills.

And the nominees are:

Caravaggio
(1986) 97m
Nigel Terry, Sean Bean
D: Derek Jarman
Controversial bio of post-Renaissance painter, known for the violence and depravity of his life and work. Gabriel Beristain's photography reproduces the artist's visual style.

Ed Wood
(1994) 120m R
Johnny Depp, Martin Landau
D: Tim Burton
Touching look at the odd life and odder career of the cross-dressing, angora-fetishist known as the worst director in movie history.

Edvard Munch
(1976) 167m
Geir Westby, Gro Fraas
D: Peter Watkins
Radical, pseudo-documentary account of radical expressionist Munch's struggle to pursue his art and maintain his sanity.

Frances
(1982) 134m
Jessica Lange, Kim Stanley
D: Graeme Clifford
Moving account of maverick '30s actress Frances Farmer, who suffered greatly after being committed to mental institutions. Lange's best work.

Lust for Life
(1956) 122m
Kirk Douglas, Anthony Quinn
D: Vincente Minnelli
Story of Vincent Van Gogh features great performance from Douglas. Quinn fine, too, as Gaugin.

Moulin Rouge
(1952) 119m
Jose Ferrer, Zsa Zsa Gabor
D: John Huston
Ferrer impressively acts on his knees as diminutive impressionist Toulouse-Lautrec. Cognac, anyone?

Prick Up Your Ears
(1987) 110m R
Gary Oldman, Alfred Molina
D: Stephen Frears
Depicts rise to fame of subversive '60s English playwright Joe Orton and his murder at the hands of his male lover.

Rosa Luxembourg
(1985) 122m
Barbara Sukowa, Daniel Olbrychski
D: Margarethe von Trotta
Stirring portrait of the feminist socialist who met with an untimely demise. Among the few video releases from great filmmaker.

Savage Messiah
(1972) 96m
Scott Antony, Dorothy Tutin
D: Ken Russell
Drama of sculptor Gaudier-Brzeska is characteristically liberated ren-

dering by Russell. Helen Mirren
awes in brief appearance as model.

And the winner is:

Malcolm X

(1992) 201m PG-13

Denzel Washington, Angela Bassett

D: Spike Lee

Stunning stylized depiction of the great black
activist who rose from a life of crime to become
a leader in the Nation of Islam. Long but worthwhile, with countless great moments.

PLENTY
(1985) 119m R
Charles Dance, Tracey Ullman, Sam Neill
D: Fred Schepisi

Overlooked drama features Streep as unfocused English woman who hopes to recapture, in civilian life, the same excitement and sense of purpose that she experienced during WWII. Her milieu, however, holds little opportunity for her. She drifts into an unhappy marriage with a straight-arrow diplomat and succumbs to depression. A brief encounter only seems to exacerbate her plight, and thus the downward spiral continues. Even perky Ullman can't help her despairing friend. Adapted from David Hare's play.

Accented Meryl:

The House of the Spirits (1993)

A Cry in the Dark (1988)

Out of Africa (1985)

Sophie's Choice (1982)

The French Lieutenant's Woman (1981)

Holocaust (1978)

Meryl in Peril:

The River Wild (1994)

Postcards from the Edge (1990)

Silkwood (1983)

Merry Meryl:

Death Becomes Her (1992)

She-Devil (1989)

Baby It's You
(1982) 105m R
Rosanna Arquette
D: John Sayles
Good girl Arquette falls for bad boy Vincent Spano who wants to be lounge singer. She goes to college, he goes to Florida. Somewhat sad, somewhat funny, somewhat like life itself.

A Chorus of Disapproval
(1989) 105m PG
Jenny Seagrove
D: Michael Winner
Introverted widower (Jeremy Irons) joins community theater and suddenly finds himself the subject of considerable female attention. Seagrove, as sexiest of the lot, delivers great comic turn.

Housekeeping
(1987) 117m PG
Christine Lahti
D: Bill Forsyth
Lahti is eccentric, free-spirited woman who becomes guardian to her two nieces in 1950s Oregon. The town does not approve. Poignant depiction of what it's like outside the norm.

Monika
(1952) 96m
Harriet Andersson
D: Ingmar Bergman
Bad girl and good boy (Lars Ekborg) leave Stockholm for island seclusion and run around naked until they get hungry and steal a roast beef. Then they go home. Then they grow angry.

One Deadly Summer
(1983) 134m R
Isabelle Adjani
D: Jean Becker
Seemingly deranged woman uses sex as pastime while hunting men who raped her mother years earlier. Unsettling, unforgettable.

Pennies from Heaven
(1981) 107m R
Bernadette Peters
D: Herbert Ross
Comedy in which obnoxious music salesman (Steve Martin) drags wholesome schoolteacher into poverty and degradation during Depression. Stunning lip-synched music sequences.

The Rapture
(1991) 100m R
Mimi Rogers
D: Michael Tolkin
Telephone operator wallowing in sexual activity changes life and falls in with bizarre Christian sect who believe that Christ's return is imminent. The price for eternal bliss proves high.

Stranger Than Paradise
(1984) 90m R
Eszter Balint
D: Jim Jarmusch
Hungarian woman arrives in NYC, falls in with lazy relative and his lazy friend (Richard Edson, John Lurie). They drive to Cleveland to meet Aunt Lottie. Then they have other adventures.

Best Male Performances That Oscar Ignored

Barton Fink
(1991) 116m R
John Turturro
D: Joel Coen
Socially conscious playwright goes mad in Hollywood hotel. But he's normal compared to his neighbor (John Goodman), a truly hellish traveling salesman. Judy Davis stays ahead of them both.

Batman
(1989) 126m PG-13
Jack Nicholson
D: Tim Burton
Jack's Joker is a truly wild and crazy guy. The rest of the movie, though, is like a fuzzy, bad dream.

The Day of the Locust
(1975) 140m R
Donald Sutherland
D: John Schlesinger
Moronic accountant, lusting after dim, amoral actress in '30s Hollywood, decides to stomp swinish child instead.

Do the Right Thing
(1989) 120m R
Giancarlo Esposito
D: Spike Lee
Uncompromising comedy about a hot day in a Brooklyn ghetto. Entire cast shines but Esposito stands out as an unlikely rabblerouser.

The Emperor Jones
(1933) 72m
Paul Robeson
D: Dudley Murphy
Good news: Railroad porter escapes a chain gang and becomes ruler of Haiti. Bad news: The natives are restless.

The Godfather III
(1990) 170m R
Al Pacino
D: Francis Ford Coppola
Michael Corleone loosens up a bit and actually tells a joke at one point. Ultimately a tragedy, Pacino makes us feel all the pain of a man who sacrifices himself for his family and, inevitably, ends up sacrificing his family as well.

Hamlet
(1990) 135m PG
Mel Gibson
D: Franco Zeffirelli
The role is, arguably, an actor's greatest challenge, and Mel delivers the performance of a lifetime. If you don't like this, you don't like Shakespeare.

Henry: Portrait of a Serial Killer
(1990) 90m X
Michael Rooker
D: John McNaughton
Disgusting, stomach-turning tale about incredibly vicious killer. Rooker gives everything in unappealing role.

House of Games
(1987) 102m R
Joe Mantegna
D: David Mamet
Con artist realizes the opportunity of a lifetime when a psychiatrist shows an interest in his profession.

MONKEY BUSINESS
(1952) 97m
Ginger Rogers, Marilyn Monroe
D: Howard Hawks

One of Grant's lesser known comedies casts him as a scientist who consumes a fountain-of-youth potion and behaves as a preening teen and, later, as a demanding child. Highlights include public-pool sequence in which Grant poses as master of diving board. In another outrageous episode, he dons Indian garb and helps neighborhood children take an adult captive. Peak, though, is boardroom scene in which he hides under table and demands a nickel. Rogers and Monroe are both fine too.

Comic Cary:

The Awful Truth (1937)

Bringing Up Baby (1938)

Holiday (1938)

His Girl Friday (1940)

My Favorite Wife (1940)

The Philadelphia Story (1940)

Arsenic and Old Lace (1944)

The Bachelor and the Bobby-Soxer (1947)

Mr. Blandings Builds His Dream House (1948)

I Was a Male War Bride (1949)

Indiscreet (1958)

That Touch of Mink (1962)

Suave Leading Man:

Notorious (1946)

To Catch a Thief (1955)

An Affair to Remember (1957)

Houseboat (1958)

North by Northwest (1959)

Charade (1963)

17

Mr. Smith Goes to Washington
(1939) 130m
James Stewart, Jean Arthur
D: Frank Capra
Naive hero gets himself elected and finds–surprise!–corruption in our capital! Is a slamming speech, full of outrage and idealism, pending?

The Wizard of Oz
(1939) 101m
Judy Garland, Margaret Hamilton
D: Victor Fleming
Midwestern girl survives tornado only to find herself in magical world where a scarecrow walks and talks and monkeys fly. You do know all this already, don't you?

The Grapes of Wrath
(1940) 129m
Henry Fonda, Jane Darwell
D: John Ford
Sobering saga about earnest poor folk enduring hardships in America's heartland during the Depression.

The Maltese Falcon
(1941) 101m
Humphrey Bogart, Mary Astor
D: John Huston
It's a carving of a bird, and the stuff that dreams are made of. Sam Spade is on the case, along with a deceitful woman, a loquacious fat man, and a weasly gunsel.

Meet John Doe
(1941) 123m
Gary Cooper, Barbara Stanwyck
D: Frank Capra
Drifter consents to reporter's scam and finds that people just don't care anymore. What better way to protest than by leaping to one's death on a snowy night?

Casablanca
(1942) 102m PG
Humphrey Bogart, Ingrid Bergman
D: Michael Curtiz
Hard guy with a heart of gold decides to risk everything to help an old flame. Cinematic equivalent of selling swampland in Jersey, but ya gotta love it.

On the Waterfront
(1954) 108m
Marlon Brando, Lee J. Cobb
D: Elia Kazan
Punchy dockworker decides to cooperate with feds investigating corruption. This one is a contender!

The Godfather
(1972) 171m R
Marlon Brando, Al Pacino
D: Francis Ford Coppola
Greatest gangster film ever (besides its sequel), with an extraordinary cast and enough great scenes to inspire multiple viewings. "We'll get there, Pop."

Around the World in 80 Days
(1956) 178m G
David Niven, Shirley MacLaine
D: Michael Anderson, Sr.
Up until *The Player*, the acknowledged cameo over-achiever. Unflappable Victorian Englishman Phileas Fogg wagers he can circumnavigate the globe in guess how many days. More than 40 cameo star appearances help him along.

A Bridge Too Far
(1977) 175m PG
James Caan, Robert Redford
D: Richard Attenborough
Whole lot of folks turn up briefly in epic about doomed Allied plan to commandeer Dutch bridges. Caan is best of big batch.

It's a Mad, Mad, Mad, Mad World
(1964) 155m
Spencer Tracy, Sid Caesar
D: Stanley Kramer
Crowded with stars shamelessly mugging for a paycheck or a chance to preen onscreen. You'll yawn, you'll hum, you'll make frequent trips to the refrigerator. What you won't do is laugh. Even Del Lord and the three Wise Men wouldn't have saved this one.

The Last Tycoon
(1976) 123m PG
Robert De Niro, Jack Nicholson
D: Elia Kazan
Host of stars hover around vacant, supposedly brilliant film producer. Jack's steals this one big time.

The List of Adrian Messenger
(1963) 98m
George C. Scott, Kirk Douglas
D: John Huston
Killer dons variety of disguises. Various actors don disguises too. You have to find them. It's fun hunting, and the actual story is pretty good too.

The Longest Day
(1962) 179m
John Wayne, Richard Burton
D: Ken Annakin
Mass of stars assault beaches of Normandy. Film's best moment involves luckless parachutist Red Buttons!

Midway
(1976) 132m PG
Charlton Heston, Henry Fonda
D: Jack Smight
Many cameos can't help bloated WWII epic, retold through Allied and Japanese viewpoints.

The Player
(1992)123m R
Tim Robbins, Greta Scacchi
D: Robert Altman
Cynical, self-congratulatory expose of Hollywood. Lots of big stars appear briefly. Big deal.

MYSTERY TRAIN
(1989) 110m R
Nicoletta Braschi, Elizabeth Bracco
D: Jim Jarmusch

Buscemi is one of those actors you probably don't know by name but you recognize immediately as someone who enlivens whatever's he's in. This guy is a shot of adrenaline when a movie's failing and one more reason to like a movie that isn't. He really shines in *Mystery Train*, independent filmmaker Jarmusch's collection of three vignettes about foreigners visiting a Memphis hotel. In the final sequence, Buscemi appears–along with Clash rocker Joe Strummer–as a wounded thief on the lam. This guy's noticeable even as he's fading from life.

Buscemi at His Best:

Airheads (1994)

Ed and His Dead Mother (1993)

Twenty Bucks (1993)

In the Soup (1992)

Reservoir Dogs (1992)

King of New York (1990)

New York Stories (1989)

Parting Glances (1986)

And the nominees are:

Coupe de Ville
(1990) 98m PG-13
*Patrick Dempsey, Daniel Stern,
    Arye Gross*
D: Joe Roth
Estranged brothers forced by dad to
drive mom's caddy from Detroit to
Florida. They listen to lots of music,
do really zany things, and bond.

Detour
(1946) 67m
Tom Neal, Ann Savage
D: Edgar G. Ulmer
Downtrodden pianist travels cross-
country to rejoin fiancee, becomes
involved in hitchhiker's death, and
finds himself stuck with truly mean
woman.

Easy Rider
(1969) 94m R
*Peter Fonda, Dennis Hopper, Jack
    Nicholson*
D: Dennis Hopper
Bikers cruise through South and
encounter really cool girls and really bummer dudes and one really
cool dude. The bummer dudes win,
even though they can't act.

The Road to Singapore
(1940) 84m
*Bob Hope, Bing Crosby, Dorothy
    Lamour*
D: Victor Schertzinger
The one that started it all. The duo
travel to Singapore to live the good
life and wind up rescuing showgirl

Lamour. Combo of corny comedy
and Bing's singing featured 6 more
times.

Slither
(1973) 97m PG
*James Caan, Sally Kellerman,
    Peter Boyle*
D: Howard Zieff
Loony chaser in which duo searching for stolen cash are joined by
flighty looker. They're followed, and
bothered.

Travels with My Aunt
(1972) 109m PG
Maggie Smith, Alec McCowen
D: Jerome Gary
Squirrely banker is treated to whirlwind tour of Europe by rather eccentric aunt. Beats *Easy Rider's*
whirlwind tour of South.

Two for the Road
(1967) 112m
Audrey Hepburn, Albert Finney
D: Stanley Donen
Married couple reflect on their
stormy life together. Solid despite
Henry Mancini music.

Voyage in Italy
(1953) 87m
Ingrid Bergman, George Sanders
D: Roberto Rossellini
Married couple reflect on their
stormy life. Actually, they're not on
the road together too much, but at
least there's no Henry Mancini
music.

Weekend
(1967) 105m
Mireille Darc, Jean Yanne
D: Jean-Luc Godard
Paris couple embark on country drive and promptly find themselves in the longest traffic jam ever filmed. Heroine eventually launches long erotic tale.

And the winner is:

Vanishing Point

(1971) 98m PG

Barry Newman, Cleavon Little

D: Richard Sarafian

Pill-popping ex-racer agrees to deliver car from Denver to San Francisco in 15 hours. From start to finish just one big whoosh.

And God Created Woman
(1988) 98m R
Rebecca DeMornay, Vincent Spano
D: Roger Vadim
Didn't do for DeMornay what the original did for Bardot, but it'll do fine for anyone eager to appraise the former's considerable physique, which is displayed to full advantage by master flesh connoisseur Vadim.

Born Yesterday
(1993) 102m PG
Melanie Griffith, Don Johnson
D: Luis Mandoki
Critically trashed modernization of '50s classic features surprisingly appealing lead performances. And, really, has John Goodman ever been less than, well, good?

Cape Fear
(1991) 128m R
Robert De Niro, Nick Nolte
D: Martin Scorsese
1961 near-classic gassed up by Scorsese. Psycho rapist leaves the slammer and tracks lawyer who failed him years earlier. Nolte, as wimp, is funny. De Niro, as villain, is scary (and funny).

Desperate Hours
(1990) 105m R
Mickey Rourke, Anthony Hopkins, Mimi Rogers
D: Michael Cimino
Gripping tale of household held captive by killer is plenty intense, particularly with Rourke wielding the weapon. Originally a '55 Bogart thriller.

The Getaway
(1993) 110m R
Alec Baldwin, Kim Basinger, James Wood
D: Roger Donaldson
Husband-and-wife leads are plenty hot as thieving lovers fleeing the ever ominous Woods. Only Sally Struthers is missed from '72 Peckinpah original.

Intersection
(1993) 98m R
Richard Gere, Sharon Stone, Lolita Davidovich
D: Mark Rydell
Refiguring of Sautet's *Choices in Life* finds Gere filled with vague dissatisfaction despite having Stone and Davidovich as wife and lover, respectively. Long drive to nowhere.

Kiss Me Goodbye
(1982) 101m PG
Jeff Bridges, Sally Field, James Caan
D: Robert Mulligan
Bridges, as usual, is fine, and Caan shows some surprising flair for softshoe, but this is a refiguring of Brazil's steamy *Dona Flor and Her Two Husbands*, so why replace hot, hot Sonia Braga with Field or, for that matter, anyone?

Night and the City
(1992) 98m R
Robert De Niro, Jessica Lange
D: Irwin Winkler
'50's film noir classic updated. De Niro and Lange are intense. Winkler, though, is hardly Scorsese. Worth a look, however, for the performers.

The Whodunit Awards: Magnificent Mysteries

Angel Heart
(1987) 112m R
Mickey Rourke, Robert De Niro
D: Alan Parker
Erotic, violent tale of detective tracking whereabouts of vanished pop singer. Sometimes you find what you're looking for, and sometimes you wish you hadn't.

The Big Sleep
(1946) 114m
Humphrey Bogart, Lauren Bacall
D: Howard Hawks
PI falls in love with employer's older daughter while uncovering younger daughter's considerable indiscretions. Compelling despite inexplicable storyline.

Dead Again
(1991) 107m R
Kenneth Branagh, Emma Thompson
D: Kenneth Branagh
Detective discovers that amnesiac's past holds relevance to his own life. Frantic and fun from England's versatile auteur.

The Lady From Shanghai
(1948) 87m
Orson Welles, Rita Hayworth
D: Orson Welles
Dim seaman falls prey to gorgeous femme and soon finds himself embroiled in considerable mayhem. Classic finale set in hall of mirrors.

The Long Goodbye
(1973) 112m R
Elliott Gould, Nina Van Pallandt
D: Robert Altman
Characteristically offbeat genre effort finds Raymond Chandler protagonist Marlowe in contemporary West Coat setting. As usual, things are rarely what they seem.

Mirage
(1966) 108m
Gregory Peck, Diane Baker
D: Edward Dmytryk
Amnesiac struggles desperately to find the Major and uncover the meaning of Unidyne. George Kennedy is outstanding as brute with firm grasp of payback concept.

Mr. Arkadin
(1955) 99m
Orson Welles, Akim Tamiroff
D: Orson Welles
Investigator discovers too late that his employer has been less than candid. Stunning church sequence, aerial climax.

Spellbound
(1945) 111m
Gregory Peck, Ingrid Bergman
D: Alfred Hitchcock
Classic mystery concerns amnesiac posing as psychoanalyst. Dream sequence designed by Salvador Dali.

Who Framed Roger Rabbit?
(1988) 104m PG
Bob Hoskins
D: Robert Zemeckis
Vivid, freewheeling pic about seedy detective involved with loopy hare. If you don't already know about this one, you probably shouldn't bother.

And the nominees are:

The Chase
(1966) 135m
Marlon Brando, Angie Dickinson
D: Arthur Penn
Honorable sheriff tries to maintain order after fellow citizens learn that local boy has escaped prison and is in area. Exciting fare with excellent lead performances.

The China Syndrome
(1979) 123m
Jane Fonda, Jack Lemmon,
  Michael Douglas
D: James Bridges
Emotionally unbalanced executive at nuclear plant learns of concealed accident, risks his life to promote public awareness.

The Dead Zone
(1983) 104m R
Christopher Walken, Martin Sheen
D: David Cronenberg
Man gains extraordinary psychic powers thanks to near-fatal accident and tries to prevent charismatic politician from destroying the world. Chilling adaptation of Stephen King novel.

The Hunt for Red October
(1990) 137m PG
Sean Connery, Alec Baldwin
D: John McTiernan
Soviet nuclear sub turns rogue and heads for U.S. waters. High tech yarn from Tom Clancy blockbuster. Fea-

tures Baldwin as Jack Ryan (played subsequently by Harrison Ford).

The Man Who Knew Too Much
(1956) 120m PG
James Stewart, Doris Day
D: Alfred Hitchcock
Americans vacationing in Marrakesh discover their son has been kidnapped by group planning major political assassination. Que sera sera.

No Way Out
(1987) 114m R
Kevin Costner, Sean Young
D: Roger Donaldson
Naval officer investigates murder of defense secretary's gorgeous mistress. Trouble is, the officer is his own most likely suspect. Features great limo sex scene before turning intense.

Rear Window
(1954) 112m
James Stewart, Grace Kelly
D: Alfred Hitchcock
Chairbound photographer suspects neighbor of murder, then neighbor suspects that chairbound photographer hasn't been minding his own business.

The Tenant
(1976) 125m R
Roman Polanski, Isabelle Adjani
D: Roman Polanski
Callow office worker in new apartment fears that neighbors are dri-

ving him to repeat suicide of previous occupant. Look before you leap.

Twelve Angry Men
(1957) 95m
Henry Fonda, Lee J. Cobb
D: Sidney Lumet
Lone voice of reason attempts to persuade stupid, lazy fellow jurors that murder suspect might be innocent.

WarGames
(1983) 110 PG
Matthew Broderick, Ally Sheedy
D: John Badham
Computer hack challenges nation's missile-defense system to thermonuclear war. The computer plays for keeps.

And the winner is:

The Shining

(1980) 143m R

Jack Nicholson, Shelly Duvall

D: Stanley Kubrick

Funny, frightening tale of deranged writer who gets severe cabin fever when snowbound with family at otherwise empty ski lodge. Feast for eye and ear, but may wear out stomach linings.

Beetlejuice
(1988) 92m PG
Michael Keaton, Geena Davis, Alec Baldwin
D: Tim Burton
Rookie ghosts summon repulsive demon to help them chase yuppie occupants from haunted house. Bent look at afterlife is highlighted by strange sets and Keaton's warp-drive demonizing.

Dona Flor and Her Two Husbands
(1978) 106m
Sonia Braga, Jose Wilker, Mauro Mendonca
D: Bruno Barreto
Woman widowed when her philandering husband vapor locks remarries dull fellow, whereupon husband number one comes back. If you were married to Braga, you'd come back too.

Field of Dreams
(1989) 106 PG
Kevin Costner, James Earl Jones
D: Phil Alden Robinson
Farmer is inspired by inner voices to construct baseball field, whereupon dead greats show for a little fungo and games. Ray Liotta comes out of the cornfield too late to save game.

Ghost
(1990) 127m PG-13
Patrick Swayze, Demi Moore
D: Jerry Zucker
Dead husband tries to save wife from same fate. You'd think she'd be more worried about her dead husband hanging around. Whoopi Goldberg easily swipes this one as supposedly fake medium.

The Ghost and Mrs. Muir
(1947) 104m
Gene Tierney, Rex Harrison
D: Joseph L. Mankiewicz
Charming fantasy in which widow is saved from poverty by irritable ghost who dictates his seafaring experiences. Voila! A bestseller for the widow!

Rendez-vous
(1988) 82 R
Juliette Binoche, Lambert Wilson
D: Andre Techine
Actress accustomed to peddling sexual favors is plagued by reappearances of dead lover after accepting role in play he starred in years earlier. Not a comedy.

Topper
(1937) 97m
Cary Grant, Marion Kerby
D: Norman Z. McLeod
Couple dead from car accident come back to help out stuffy friend. Grant is usual master in this delightful comedy.

Truly, Madly, Deeply
(1991) 107m PG
Juliet Stevenson, Alan Rickman
D: Anthony Minghella
Woman despairing after lover's death is surprised when he returns, along with buddies like Napoleon. Touching and funny.

BLADE RUNNER

(1982) 122m R
Harrison Ford, Sean Young, Rutger Hauer
D: Ridley Scott

Los Angeles in the early 21st-century is a nightmare of rain, filth, and crime. One big departure from contemporary L.A. however, is the dangerous band of marauding replicants out for revenge against their creators. Still regrouping from the Rodney King thing, the LAPD call upon a reluctant bounty hunter specializing in replicant extermination. The chase is on. Unfortunately, at least for the bounty hunter (explaining his reluctance), the replicants possess extraordinary strength and above high-school intelligence, and turn the game into one of stalking the hunter. Simplistic sci-fi-wise plot services awesome sets and rhythmic excitement. Ford is perfect as the world weary blade runner, and Young is utterly sympathetic as a replicant longing to be human, a dream she still holds. But Hauer steals this one as the gleefully magnificent replicant out to settle a few issues.

More Futureshock:

The Handmaid's Tale (1990)
Class of 1999 (1990)
Brazil (1985)
Escape from New York (1981)
Quintet (1979)
Stalker (1979)
Rollerball (1975)
Sleeper (1973)
Zardoz (1973)
Fahrenheit 451 (1966)

Alien
(1979) 116m R
Sigourney Weaver, John Hurt
D: Ridley Scott
Ten Little Indians in space, with a murderous, ever-evolving creature roaming a space ship. Hurt's demise is particularly gut-wrenching.

Android
(1982) 80m PG
Klaus Kinski, Don Opper
D: Aaron Lipstadt
Good-natured but monotonous android discovers that his obsessive, unsettling owner is about to disconnect him. Guess which one is Kinski.

Barbarella
(1968) 98m PG
Jane Fonda, John Phillip Law
D: Roger Vadim
Space heroine goes about adventuring despite encounters with men hellbent on undressing her.

Flesh Gordon
(1972) 70m
Jason Williams, Suzanne Fields
D: Mike Light
Heroic Flesh must save Earth from evil Wang's sex ray. Amusing special effects, amazing acting.

Lifeforce
(1985) 100m R
Mathilda May, Steve Railsback
D: Tobe Hooper
Gorgeous vampire from space soon severely depletes London's supply of blood donors.

Outland
(1981) 109 R
Sean Connery, Peter Boyle
D: Peter Hyams
High Noon on Jupiter, with Connery as good guy obligated to confront baddies. Stunning sets.

Saturn 3
(1980) 88m R
Kirk Douglas, Farrah Fawcett
D: Stanley Donen
Husband-and-wife researchers have their space-station idyll undone by psychotic scientist (Harvey Keitel) manipulating killer robot. Has Keitel ever read a script he didn't like?

Total Recall
(1990) 113m R
Arnold Schwarzenegger, Sharon Stone
D: Paul Verhoeven
Construction worker on Mars discovers his memories have been implanted. He's married to sultry Stone, but wants to uncover the truth anyway. Incredible effects.

Zardoz
(1973) 105m
Sean Connery, Charlotte Rampling
D: John Boorman
Futuristic saga about class struggle on Earth. Savagery infiltrates the intellectual class and chaos ensues.

THE HIT
(1985) 105m R
Terence Stamp, Tim Roth, Laura Del Sol
D: *Stephen Frears*

Hurt's is a brooding, troubled screen presence, and that has rarely been more evident than in this quirky work about a hired killer's truly bad experience. Hurt's killer is to escort a stoolie through Spain and deliver him to the mob. The stoolie, far from showing fear, seems truly reconciled to his fate and–to the killer's annoyance–muses philosophically about the temporary nature of life. To make matters worse, the killer's youthful, obnoxious sidekick proves a nuisance, as does the buxom hostage they take on. The one is, in essence, the story of a bad hair week.

Hurt Hits:

The Field (1990)

Frankenstein Unbound (1990)

Scandal (1989)

White Mischief (1988)

After Darkness (1985)

Champions (1984)

Ninety Eighty Four (1984)

The Elephant Man (1980)

Alien (1979)

Midnight Express (1978)

The Shout (1978)

The Naked Civil Servant (1975)

And the nominees are:

Batman Returns
(1992) 126m PG-13
Michael Keaton, Michelle Pfeiffer
D: *Tim Burton*
Pfieffer excels as the seductive, leather-clad Catwoman, complete with bullwhip, while Danny DeVito is a suitably disgusting Penguin.

Cape Fear
(1961) 106m
Gregory Peck, Robert Mitchum
D: *J. Lee Thompson*
Sadistic ex-con decides to ruin life of attorney who put him in slammer. Mitchum's restrained creepiness contrasts greatly with De Niro's over-the-top performance in Scorsese remake.

A Clockwork Orange
(1971) 137m R
Malcolm McDowell, Patrick Magee
D: *Stanley Kubrick*
Futuristic tale (with equally futuristic language) about gangleader conducting minions on regular stints of rape and murder. And he's the hero! Anthony Burgess novel.

Die Hard
(1988) 114m R
Bruce Willis, Bonnie Bedelia
D: *John McTiernan*
Fiendish terrorist (Alan Rickman) overtakes high rise. Can wisecracking cop save the day and his marriage? Alas, probably. (And he did it again in the sequel.)

The Duellists
(1977) 101m PG
Keith Carradine, Harvey Keitel
D: *Ridley Scott*
Picturesque rendering of Conrad tale about upright officer tormented by unstable peer. Keitel is, of course, the latter.

In the Line of Fire
(1993) 128m R
Clint Eastwood, John Malkovich
D: *Wolfgang Petersen*
Aging Secret Service agent almost meets his match in the menancing caller who's planning to kill the Prez. Malkovich nearly steals the movie from no-bull Eastwood.

Missouri Breaks
(1976) 126m PG
Jack Nicholson, Marlon Brando
D: *Arthur Penn*
Rustlers pose as ranchers only to find themselves prey to gleeful, schizophrenic gunslinger. Brando sometimes scary, sometimes funny as hired hand.

Robin Hood: Prince of Thieves
(1991) 144m PG-13
Kevin Costner, Morgan Freeman
D: *Kevin Reynolds*
Costner woodenly attacks title role, speaking with rare medieval-California surfer dude accent. Real treat is way over-the-top Alan Rickman as the naughty Sheriff of Nottingham.

Romeo Is Bleeding
(1993) 110m R
Gary Oldman, Lena Olin
D: Peter Medak
Crooked cop tries to set up hired killer for murder. Big mistake. She exacts considerable revenge.

Shane
(1953) 117m
Alan Ladd, Brandon de Wilde
D: George Stevens
Retired gunslinger comes to aid of family harassed by land baron's despicable henchman. Jack Palance wears only black.

And the winner is:

Dirty Harry

(1971) 103m R

Clint Eastwood, Andrew Robinson

D: Don Siegel

Hardnosed cop stalks psychopath who preys on children. Robinson delivers the definitive portrait of villainy.

The Adventures of Robin Hood
(1938) 102m
Erroll Flynn, Olivia de Havilland
D: Michael Curtiz
Steal from the rich, give to the poor! Flynn has never been more dashing, and Basil Rathbone never more evil. Stunning sword fighting sequences. You too, will want to effortlessly engage in spirited repartee while fighting a castle full of the enemy.

The African Queen
(1951) 105m
Humphrey Bogart, Katharine Hepburn
D: John Huston
Boozy sea captain offers to escort prim missionary, ends up taking on a German gunboat, fighting with passenger, and finding romance.

Butch Cassidy and the Sundance Kid
(1969) 110m PG
Paul Newman, Robert Redford
D: George Roy Hill
Irascible outlaws can't quite get on top of their profession. Fine entertainment despite B.J. Thomas interlude. Strother Martin rules as irascible miner.

From Here to Eternity
(1953) 118m
Burt Lancaster, Deborah Kerr, Montgomery Clift
D: Fred Zinneman
Dramatic portraits of various individuals at Pearl Harbor during time of Japanese attack. High points include Frank Sinatra's death at hands of brutal Ernest Borgnine.

Oh yeah, there's also a sandy clinch between Lancaster and Kerr.

Gone with the Wind
(1939) 231m
Vivien Leigh, Clark Gable
D: Victor Fleming
Civil War, southern style. There's love, there's danger, there's adventure, there's a vow inspired by an uprooted vegetable. C'mon, give a damn.

Harvey
(1950) 104m
James Stewart, Josephine Hull
D: Henry Koster
Good-natured alcoholic regularly confides in invisible rabbit. Good-natured viewers will confide in alcohol.

The Lady Eve
(1941) 93m
Barbara Stanwyck, Henry Fonda
D: Preston Sturges
Female con artist falls in love with her dimwitted victim, a wealthy beer tycoon and writer whose book is *Are Snakes Necessary*. Yes, this is a comedy and a notable one by the master Sturges.

Love Is a Many Splendored Thing
(1955) 102m
William Holden, Jennifer Jones
D: Henry King
Married war correspondent falls in love with Hong Kong doctor after WWII. Holden has never been better, but you'd better watch this one near a box of tissues.

Mr. Deeds Goes to Town
(1936) 118m
Gary Cooper, Jean Arthur
D: Frank Capra
Likeable guy inherits $20 million and promptly donates it to the needy. Then he becomes really likeable guy. Hardnosed reporter decides to expose hero and ends up in love. They don't call it Capracorn for nothing.

Paths of Glory
(1957) 86m
Kirk Douglas, Adolphe Menjou
D: Stanley Kubrick
Self-inflated officer imposes suicidal strategy on troops during WWI, then demands executions when plan fails. Douglas is outstanding as the officer who knows the truth.

Picnic
(1955) 113m
William Holden, Kim Novak
D: Joshua Logan
Studly guy roams into town, wins love of friend's girl. Other women in town experience difficulty keeping their tongues off the pavement.

Singin' in the Rain
(1952) 103m
Gene Kelly, Debbie Reynolds, Donald O'Connor
D: Gene Kelly, Stanley Donen
Perhaps the greatest musical ever made. If only all fun movies were actually this much fun.

Star Wars
(1977) 121m PG
Mark Hamill, Harrison Ford, Carrie Fisher
D: George Lucas
Battle between good and evil is waged yet again, with plenty of breathtaking adventure to stir even the stillest of hearts. Has good sequels too.

The Treasure of the Sierra Madre
(1948) 126m
Humphrey Bogart, Walter Huston
D: John Huston
Greedy prospectors combat each other and corrupt lawmen while searching for gold in Mexico. "Badges? We don't need no stinking badges!"

The Way We Were
(1973) 118m PG
Robert Redford, Barbra Streisand
D: Sydney Pollack
Boy next door falls for Jewish radical while in college. They marry, but don't really mix. You'll laugh, you'll cry, you'll check your watch.

Yankee Doodle Dandy
(1942) 126m
James Cagney, Joan Leslie
D: Michael Curtiz
Gangster icon Cagney displays his versatility as Broadway's song-and-dance legend George M. Cohan.

An American Werewolf in London

(1981) 97m R
David Naughton, Griffin Dunne
D: *John Landis*
Werewolf's victims keep turning up in various stages of decay. Maybe it's a comedy.

Blood Feast

(1963) 70m
Connie Mason, Thomas Wood
D: *Herschell Gordon Lewis*
Demented caterer butchers women at behest of Egyptian goddess.

Creepers

(1985) 82m R
Jennifer Connelly, Donald Pleasence
D: *Dario Argento*
Nightmarish gorefest finds comely Connelly immersed in blood pit replete with decayed corpses and ravenous maggots. Welcome to L.A.

Desperate Living

(1977) 90m
Jean Hill, Mink Stole
D: *John Waters*
Obese maid crushes lewd employer, flees to Mordville, land of truly despicable degenerates. Should sex with a mailman really be punishable by rabies injection?

Natural Born Killers

(1994) 1991m R
Woody Harrelson, Juliette Lewis
D: *Oliver Stone*
Mass-murdering couple become pop culture icons thanks to slavering press. Comic book style prevents violence from being as realistically disgusting as you may fear.

Pink Flamingos

(1972) 95m
Divine, Mink Stole
D: *John Waters*
Legendary depiction of demented brood living in secluded trailer. Bestiality, rape, coprophilia, and one singularly talented fellow who mimes *Surfer Bird* with his anus.

Sante Sangre

(1990) 123m NC-17
Axel Jodorowsky, Sabrina Dennison
D: *Alejandro Jodorowsky*
Devoted son serves as his mother's arms and eventually kills for her. Movie may be too close to home for some viewers.

True Romance

(1993) 116m R
Christian Slater, Patricia Arquette
D: *Tony Scott*
Inept duo skip town with a suitcase full of Mob heroin and head out to L.A. Horrific violence, including a shoot-out to end all shoot-outs, mixed with very black humor. Quentin Tarantino script.

2000 Maniacs

(1964) 75m
Thomas Wood, Connie Mason
D: *Herschell Gordon Lewis*
Ghost town of Confederate dead take revenge on trespassing Yankees. Lewis is the master of creative dismemberment.

Basic Instinct
(1992) 122m R
Michael Douglas, Sharon Stone
D: Paul Verhoeven
Burned-out cop falls for manipulative bisexual writer who may also be mutilating sexual partners with an icepick. Male Buttocks Alert posted.

The Bitch
(1978) 90m R
Joan Collins
D: Gerry O'Hara
Beautiful divorcee indulges herself materially and sexually, tormenting various men in process. Collins forever young.

Excalibur
(1981) 140m R
Nigel Terry, Helen Mirren
D: John Boorman
Sword-and-sorcery epic hums along nicely until arrival of Mirren's Morgana, an evil sorceress who sexually accosts her brother, then raises a son to kill off her same sibling. Ahhh, the good old days.

Jezebel
(1938) 105m
Bette Davis, Henry Fonda
D: William Wyler
Southern spitfire puts her fiance through the paces until he actually starts to die.

Mommie Dearest
(1981) 129m PG
Faye Dunaway
D: Frank Perry
Dunaway is scary as actress Joan Crawford, who was rather frightening anyway. "No more wire hangers!"

The Odd Couple
(1968) 106m G
Jack Lemmon, Walter Matthau
D: Gene Saks
War rages when divorced men become roommates. Trouble is, one is a slob, the other, a nagging neatness fanatic. Guess which one is Lemmon.

The Ref
(1993) 97m R
Judy Davis, Denis Leary, Kevin Spacey
D: Ted Demme
Bungling burglar stumbles into domestic war between obnoxious couple. Davis runs riot as heartless wife.

Reflections in a Golden Eye
(1967) 109m
Marlon Brando, Elizabeth Taylor
D: John Huston
Emotionally repressed army officer strays from his abusive wife to watch troops shower. Big Marlon intimidated by Bigger Liz.

Who's Afraid of Virginia Woolf?
(1966) 127m
Richard Burton, Elizabeth Taylor
D: Mike Nichols
Young couple are witness to warfare between tired professor and his heartily abusive wife. Taylor's greatest performance. Burton's too.

And the nominees are:

Body Heat
(1981) 113m R
William Hurt, Kathleen Turner
D: Lawrence Kasdan
Dimwitted lawyer becomes involved with scheming seductress during Florida heat wave. Torrid despite ludicrous finale.

Dark Obsession
(1990) 96m NC-17
Gabriel Byrne, Amanda Donohoe
D: Nick Broomfield
Brit twit involved in hit-and-run fatality has fantasies in which his wife is unfaithful. Strong rapport between leads.

Devil in the Flesh
(1986) 110m X
Maruschka Detmers, Federico Pitzalis
D: Marco Bellocchio
Schoolboy becomes sexually involved with voluptuous, rather mad older woman. Unnerving drama features talented Detmers in explicit sequence.

Hot Spot
(1990) 120m R
Don Johnson, Virginia Madsen, Jennifer Connelly
D: Dennis Hopper
Stud drifter has affair with both boss's eternally heated wife and fetching younger gal. Then he decides to rob a bank.

I Love You
(1981) 104m R
Sonia Braga, Paulo Cesar Prelo
D: Arnaldo Jabor
Man and woman undertake cat-and-mouse sexual shenanigans in room with a view. Braga in peak form.

Jamon Jamon
(1993) 95m
Penelope Cruz, Stefania Sandrelli
D: Bigas Luna
Girl falls in love with boy who is still hot for her mom who is his father's ex-lover. Boy's mother falls for stud hired to seduce son's girlfriend. Stud just wants a motorcycle. Title translates to "Ham, Ham" which the stud eats to enhance sexual prowess.

9 1/2 Weeks
(1986) 114m R
Mickey Rourke, Kim Basinger
D: Adrian Lyne
Chance meeting between business executive and art-gallery worker soon turns into sado-masochistic play. Inspiring despite lifeless leads. Strong use of refrigerator contents.

Tokyo Decadence
(1993) 92m NC-17
Miho Nikaido, Sayoko Amano
D: Ryu Murakami
Attractive young woman works as prostitute specializing in sado-masochism. Contains some rather weird moments, including classic strangulation scene.

Tropic of Cancer
(1970) 87m NC-17
Rip Torn, Ellen Burstyn
D: Joseph Strick
Drama based on Henry Miller's autobiographical account of sexual hijinx in 1920s Paris.

And the winner is:

Last Tango in Paris

(1973) 130m X

Marlon Brando, Maria Schneider

D: Bernardo Bertolucci

Cynical, over-the-hill American with dead wife uses young woman for sex, then finds himself falling in love with her. Brando's performance is among medium's finest.

Betty Blue
(1986) 121m R
Beatrice Dalle, Jean-Hughes Anglade
D: *Jean-Jacques Beineix*
Striking tale about promising writer and his love for a deranged woman. Film opens with vivid coupling, but focus eventually shifts from sexuality to sanity.

Don't Look Now
(1973) 110m R
Julie Christie, Donald Sutherland
D: *Nicolas Roeg*
Disturbing, horrific tale of a husband and wife overcoming their child's death. Unnerving mood subsides only during vividly convincing love scene between leads.

Five Easy Pieces
(1970) 98m R
Jack Nicholson, Susan Anspach
D: *Bob Rafelson*
Underachieving pianist turned oil worker forsakes job and pregnant girlfriend for visit to dysfunctional family. But first he engages the sexually aggressive Sally Struthers.

Matador
(1986) 90m
Assumpta Serna, Nacho Martinez
D: *Pedro Almodovar*
Murderous beauty and sexually deranged matador find each other and proceed to undertake suicidal sex. Among director's more intense efforts.

Not of This Earth
(1988) 92m R
Traci Lords
D: *Jim Wynorski*
Aliens cavort and circulate among earthlings, with striking slo-mo scene of gorgeous Lords soaring across screen.

The Sailor Who Fell from Grace with the Sea
(1976) 105m R
Sarah Miles, Kris Kristofferson
D: *Lewis John Carlino*
Forlorn woman is sexually reawakened when lanky sailor enters life she shares with her peculiar child.

Shampoo
(1975) 112m R
Warren Beatty, Julie Christie
D: *Hal Ashby*
Recklessly promiscuous hairdresser juggles affairs while trying to further career. Christie has unique way of showing her affection for hero during political banquet.

Sweet Movie
(1974) 120m
Carol Laure, Pierre Clementi
D: *Dusan Makavejev*
Strange take on sex and politics finds two characters together in massive mound of sugar. Later, Laure squirms naked while doused with chocolate.

Tie Me Up, Tie Me Down
(1990) 105m NC-17
Victoria Abril, Antonio Banderas
D: *Pedro Almodovar*
Former porn actress is abducted and held captive by former mental patient. She, eventually, finds herself drawn to him sexually. Can true love be far behind?

Roman Polanski,
Idiosyncratic Artist Most Likely to Go Abroad

BITTER MOON
(1992) 135m R
*Peter Coyote, Emmanuelle Seigner,
Hugh Grant, Kristin Scott Thomas*

No matter what the nature of his material—be it literary adaptation, conventional genre piece, or original work—Polanski manages to share his own complex and skewed perception. That peculiar vision is quite evident in *Bitter Moon*, where love leads to hate and liberation to enslavement. The plot is simple: A wheelchair bound, cynical writer confides in a straight-arrow Brit while on an ocean liner. The writer relates the circumstances of his relationship to a woman who develops from fun-loving innocent to oversexed wife to abuse victim to vengeful sadist. A comedy about cruelty, this may be one of Polanski's most definitive works, though it sure ain't for everyone.

Roman's Remains:

Death and the Maiden (1994)
Frantic (1988)
Pirates (1986)
Tess (1980)
The Tenant (1976)
Chinatown (1974)
Diary of Forbidden Dreams (1973)

Macbeth (1971)
Rosemary's Baby (1968)
The Fearless Vampire Killers (1967)
Cul de Sac (1966)
Repulsion (1965)
Knife in the Water (1962)
The Fat and the Lean (1961)
Two Men & a Wardrobe (1958)

And the nominees are:

American Gigolo
(1979) 117m R
Richard Gere, Lauren Hutton
D: Paul Schrader
High-priced fellow roaming Beverly Hills is framed for murder and only a state senator's wife can help him. Women love the venetian blind scene.

Crimes of Passion
(1984) 101m
Kathleen Turner, Anthony Perkins
D: Ken Russell
Steadfast fashion designer by day is kinky prostitute by night. She's also subject of deranged street preacher's fantasies, and it's a Russell adventure.

Hussy
(1980) 95m R
Helen Mirren, John Shea
D: Matthew Chapman
Prostitute and boyfriend become embroiled in intrigue with thugs and drug dealers.

Klute
(1971) 114m R
Jane Fonda, Donald Sutherland
D: Alan J. Pakula
Cynical hooker Fonda is stalked by killer, Sutherland is the cop who tries to save her.

McCabe and Mrs. Miller
(1971) 121m R
Warren Beatty, Julie Christie
D: Robert Altman
Buffoon opens brothel and soon finds himself beset by thugs proposing undesirable buy-out package. Christie is costly, practical madame with penchant for opium.

Midnight Cowboy
(1969) 113m R
Jon Voight, Dustin Hoffman
D: John Schlesinger
Naive Texan arrives in NYC to get rich as sex hustler. He gets stuck with tubercular geek instead.

Pretty Baby
(1978) 109m R
Brooke Shields, Susan Sarandon
D: Louis Malle
Sarandon steals this one as fetching, occasionally sympathetic hooker in turn-of-the-century New Orleans bordello. Shields plays pre-adolescent prostitute.

Pretty Woman
(1990) 117m R
Julia Roberts, Richard Gere
D: Garry Marshall
Plucky prostitute wins love of stuffy businessman. Hackneyed, improbable tale redeemed by game leads and Laura San Giacomo as Roberts' hooker pal.

Risky Business
(1983) 99m R
Tom Cruise, Rebecca DeMornay
D: Paul Brickman
Home Alone in high school. Cruise dances in underwear, smashes dad's Porsche, hires call girl, has sex on subway–and finds himself in deep water. Sometimes you just have to say, "what the heck."

The Winter of Our Dreams
(1982) 89m
Judy Davis, Bryan Brown
D: John Duigan
Addict/hooker befriends dour bookshop owner. Vivid, seamy drama with fine work from Davis.

And the winner is:

Whore

(1991) 92m

Theresa Russell, Antonio Vargas

D: Ken Russell

Gritty, unflinching drama of cynical prostitute and how she got that way. Not easy viewing.

Beneath the Valley of the Ultravixens
(1979) 90m
Kitten Natavidad, Ann Marie
D: Russ Meyer
Sex comedy concerns the more loopy experiences of various women possessing overpowering anatomical parts. Meyer's most distinguished, enthralling effort.

Big Bird Cage
(1972) 93m
Pam Grier, Candace Roman
D: Jack Hill
Another depiction of the steamy goings on in the slammer. Once again women shower repeatedly and wrestle each other.

Big Doll House
(1971) 93 R
Judy Brown, Pam Grier
D: Jack Hill
Hard core chicks kicking keester in this prison epic. Grier, as usual, is an astounding eyeful.

The Bikini Car Wash Company
(1990) 87 R
Suzanne Browne, Kristie Ducati
D: Ed Hansen
Here's something different: Outrageously attractive women hit on moneymaking scheme that enables them to both humiliate lecherous idiots and disrobe regularly.

Caged Heat
(1974) 83m R
Juanita Brown, Barbara Steele
D: Jonathan Demme
Director Demme's debut is not the usual babes-behind-bars pic–this time, the gals are true thinkers who unite to defy their less appealing oppressors. Steele is, as usual, disturbing.

Hollywood Hot Tubs
(1984) 103m R
Donna McDaniel, Edy Williams
D: Chuck Vincent
Impressive portrayal of West Coast living, with forthright women realizing success by repairing the hot tubs of the rich and famous.

H.O.T.S.
(1979) 95m R
Susan Kiger, Danny Bonaduce
D: Gerald Seth Sinddell
Stunning, insightful depiction of life in the world today, replete with enterprising women who show considerable pluck and fortitude.

Supervixens
(1975) 105m
Shari Eubank, Charles Napier
D: Russ Meyer
Gas station attendant is wrongly accused of murder and goes on the run. He then meets several staggering disproportionate women. Meyers' masterpiece.

Women in Cell Block 7
(1984) 94m
Anita Strindberg, Eve Czerneys
D: Rino Di Silvestro
Grim drama in which staggeringly fetching women are subjected to abuse by loathsome prison officials. Power to the people!

COFFY

(1973) 91m R
Booker Bradshaw, Robert DoQui
D: Jack Hill

In Blaxploitation films of the 70s a tough hero or heroine, frequently dwelling in a less-than-desirable urban area, would usually seek revenge against vicious hoodlums, drug-dealers, mobsters, or any combination thereof responsible for a loved one's demise. Grier dominated this genre in a series of 'hood epics in which she would, inevitably, go undercover to seek justice. *Coffy* is a fine example of Grier at her vengeful, butt-kicking best. Here she feigns drug addiction to familiarize herself with the despicable dealers who killed her sister. An overpowering screen presence, Grier's tough and gorgeous. Stay on her good side.

More Grier–Seventies-Style:

The Big Doll House (1971)
The Big Bird Cage (1972)
Twilight People (1972)
Naked Warriors (1973)
Scream, Blacula, Scream (1973)

Foxy Brown (1974)
Bucktown (1975)
Friday Foster (1975)
Sheba, Baby (1975)
Drum (1976)
Greased Lightning (1977)

Cobra
(1986) 87m R
Sylvester Stallone, Brigitte Nielsen
D: George P. Cosmatos
Strong, silent law enforcer protects gorgeous model from squad of hell-bent killers. Low on emotion but high on pulsating pecs.

Enter the Dragon
(1973) 98m R
Bruce Lee, John Saxon
D: Robert Clouse
Lee is recruited by Brits to track dangerous opium smugglers operating in Hong Kong. Extraordinary fight sequences feature range of martial arts.

Fists of Fury
(1973) 102m R
Bruce Lee
D: Lo Wei
Genre master Lee breaks vow of nonviolence and tracks his teacher's drug-dealing killers.

Half a Loaf of Kung Fu
(1985) 98m
Jackie Chan
D: Jackie Chan
The Michael Jordan of chop-socky, Chan plays a dedicated bodyguard determined to recover a stolen statue and maim its temporary owners.

Hard-Boiled
(1992) 126m
Chow Yun-fat
D: John Woo
Fast and furious action as a police officer infiltrates band of murderous gun smugglers. Incredible violence has never been rendered with greater artistry.

Hard Target
(1993) 97m R
Jean-Claude Van Damme
D: John Woo
Merchant seaman risks life to rescue beautiful damsel. In process, he severely thrashes multitude of vicious villians.

Hard to Kill
(1989) 96m R
Steven Seagal, Kelly Le Brock
D: Bruce Malmuth
Expressionless policeman is left, understandably enough, for dead by gun-wielding fiends. But, eventually, he prepares to destroy his attackers.

Raw Deal
(1986) 106m R
Arnold Schwarzenegger, Kathryn Harrold
D: John Irvin
Muscular FBI agent infiltrates mob and generally kicks considerable hind quarter.

Red Sonja
(1985) 89m PG-13
Arnold Schwarzenegger, Brigitte Nielsen
D: Richard Fleischer
Sword-and-sorcerer action finds muscular warrior uniting with physically imposing warrioress to thwart evil, somewhat muscular queen. Even Arnold gets in on the cleavage-a-thon action.

POINT OF NO RETURN
(1993) 109m R
Gabriel Byrne, Harvey Keitel
D: *John Badham*

Fonda, the only one bearing the illustrious acting name that stills seems to have any intelligence, is among the most savvy actresses to come along in recent years. She plays bright, she plays bratty, she plays bright and bratty, she plays brains. Here, Fonda plays dangerous, starring as a former drug burnout who is condemned to death but receives a reprieve by agreeing to serve as a government assassin. She becomes increasingly humanized during training, and by the time she's turned loose she's a reluctant, but resourceful hitter. This one's both exciting and intelligent. It's based, by the way, on the French hit *La Femme Nikita*.

Lookin' for Love:
Camilla (1994)
It Could Happen to You (1994)
Bodies, Rest & Motion (1993)
Singles (1992)
Shag: The Movie (1989)
Jacob Have I Loved (1988)

Lookin' for Something Else:
The Road to Wellville (1994)
Little Buddha (1993)
Single White Female (1992)
Frankenstein Unbound (1990)
The Godfather, Part 3 (1990)
Leather Jackets (1990)
Strapless (1990)
Scandal (1989)
Aria (1988)

And the nominees are:

The Blues Brothers
(1980) 133m R
John Belushi, Dan Aykroyd
D: John Landis
Jake and Elwood Blues attempt to raise money for an orphanage by putting their old band back together. An excuse to run amuck around Chicago.

Breathless
(1983) 105m R
Richard Gere, Valerie Kaprisky
D: Jim McBridge
Quirky remake of Godard classic has Gere as fleeing cop killer disguised in formal bowling attire. Kaprisky, wearing less, is fetching too.

The French Connection
(1971) 102m R
Gene Hackman, Roy Scheider
D: William Friedkin
Tough narcotics cops track major crime operation. Wild car chase merely one of many thrilling scenes in brutally realistic masterwork.

The Fugitive
(1993) 127m PG-13
Harrison Ford, Tommy Lee Jones
D: Andrew Davis
Doctor goes on the run after he's wrongly convicted of wife's murder. Jones is the ruthless cop chasing him down. Exhilarating, exhausting, exciting.

The Gauntlet
(1977) 111m R
Clint Eastwood, Sondra Locke
D: Clint Eastwood
Barely competent cop tries to escort prostitute witness to mob trial. Among Clint's more freewheeling efforts. Be the first to yell, "Shoot the tire."

Pee Wee's Big Adventure
(1985) 92m PG
Paul Reubens, Elizabeth Daily
D: Tim Burton
Wild, wild comedy about severe nerd desperate to recover his stolen bicycle. Barroom encounter with motorcyclists is classic, as is concluding film-within-film sequence.

The Road Warrior
(1982) 95m R
Mel Gibson
D: George Miller
Post-apocalyptic Australia is beset by bands of violent, roving marauders in search of fuel. Gibson's a reluctant, equally violent hero. Sequel to *Mad Max*.

Run
(1991) 91m R
Patrick Dempsey, Kelly Preston
D: Geoff Burrowes
Undeservedly obscure pic about student who runs into considerable trouble while transporting auto. This one rarely slows.

Smokey and the Bandit
(1977) 96m PG
Burt Reynolds, Jackie Gleason
D: Hal Needham
Good ol' boy wagers that he can
haul beer from Texas to Atlanta
in record time. Ludicrously grim cop
tries to stop him.

And the winner is:

Bullitt

(1968) 105m PG

Steven McQueen, Robert Vaughn

D: Peter Yates

Tough cop must protect endangered witness
for 48 hours. Contains the greatest car chase of
any Hollywood production.

Death Wish

(1974) 93m R
Charles Bronson
D: Michael Winner

Blood-crazed retaliator can't seem to leave his apartment without coming upon seedy criminals begging for punishment. Creative use of penny rolls and socks.

The Killer

(1990) 110m R
Chow Yun-fat
D: John Woo

Gangster gunman wants to retire but then agrees to one last hit. Considerable mayhem ensues in this masterful effort from genre master Woo.

The Long Riders

(1980) 110m R
Keach Brothers, Quaid Brothers,
* Carradine Brothers*
D: Walter Hill

3 sets of outlaw brothers evoke considerable mayhem before being tracked by still another set of siblings. Notable for bloody, slow-motion shootouts accompanied by slowed-down sounds.

Pat Garrett and Billy the Kid

(1973) 106m
James Coburn, Kris Kristofferson
D: Sam Peckinpah

Elegiac reflection on the waning West still provides considerable gunplay for those so inclined. Highlights include nonshootout between Kristofferson and genre regular Jack Elam.

Ran

(1985) 160m R
Tatsuya Nakadai, Meiko Harada
D: Akira Kurosawa

Masterful reworking of King Lear features some of the most spectacular battle scenes ever filmed. And the villainess meets a particularly grim demise.

Reservoir Dogs

(1992) 100m R
Tim Roth, Michael Madsen, Harvey
* Keitel*
D: Quentin Tarantino

Gut-shot thief lies in ever-widening pool of blood and gets to watch fellow crook with psychotic leanings slice the ear off captured cop, while dancing to Stealers Wheel *Stuck in the Middle with You.* Nuff said.

Scarface

(1983) 170m R
Al Pacino, Michelle Pfeiffer
D: Brian DePalma

Cuban criminal comes to Miami and quickly takes over crime operation. Bloody action, over-the-top acting.

The Wild Bunch

(1969) 145m R
William Holden, Ernest Borgnine
D: Sam Peckinpah

Aging outlaws attempt one last score. Classic western spends more bullets than both world wars.

PULP FICTION

(1994) 153m R
Samuel L. Jackson, Uma Thurman
D: *Quentin Tarantino*

Travolta triumphs as heroin-addicted hitman Vincent Vega in Tarantino's pop culture trilogy of violence, romance, and redemption. A clever look at everyday life on the fringes of mainstream society. And yes, the disco-meister has not forgotten his dancing skills.

Terrific Travolta:

Look Who's Talking (1989)
Blow Out (1981)
The Boy in the Plastic Bubble (1976)
Carrie (1976)

Trashy Travolta:

Look Who's Talking Now (1993)
Look Who's Talking, Too (1990)
Perfect (1985)
Two of a Kind (1983)

Twistin' Travolta:

Shout (1991)
Staying Alive (1983)
Urban Cowboy (1980)
Grease (1978)
Saturday Night Fever (1977)

Blood Song
(1982) 90m
Frankie Avalon
D: Alan J. Levi
Escaped mental patient stalks woman after she sees him burying murder victim. Surf's up.

Charro!
(1969) 98m G
Elvis Presley
D: Charles Marquis Warren
Western drama featuring the King as a reformed outlaw harassed by former mates. You'll root for the mates.

The Conqueror
(1956) 111m
John Wayne, Susan Hayward
D: Dick Powell
The Duke as Genghis Khan? No wonder the government was detonating nuclear weapons near the film sites. Guaranteed: Offers the worst delivery of the worst dialogue in any major Hollywood production.

Guys and Dolls
(1955) 150m
Marlon Brando, Frank Sinatra
D: Joseph L. Mankiewicz
Musical in which you actually want Sinatra to sing, because it means that Brando isn't. Not as bad as it seems, but at 2 1/2 hours it offers plenty of small tortures.

The Pride and the Passion
(1957) 132m
Cary Grant, Frank Sinatra
D: Stanley Kramer
Resistance troops fight for freedom in 1810 Spain. Grant is merely wrong as a military officer, but Sinatra is woeful as a Spanish peasant.

Suddenly
(1954) 75m
Frank Sinatra, Sterling Hayden
D: Lewis Allen
Sinatra is a hired killer who establishes sniper's lair in hick family's home, then waits for president's train to arrive. Unlikely casting works here–Sinatra is truly intense as the killer.

The Teahouse of the August Moon
(1956) 123m
Marlon Brando, Glenn Ford
D: Daniel Mann
Brando mugs and prances as Oriental moron. Makes you think the Emperor's forces should have flown past Pearl Harbor and done Hollywood instead.

The Young Lions
(1958) 167m
Marlon Brando, Montgomery Clift, Dean Martin
D: Edward Dmytryk
Follows 3 soldiers during final days of WWII. Unlikely casting strikes paydirt twice: Brando is moving as Nazi officer, and Martin steals entire picture as plucky GI. Clift, as usual, is fine too.

And the nominees are:

Cleopatra
(1963) 246m
*Elizabeth Taylor, Richard Burton,
Rex Harrison
D: Joseph L. Mankiewicz*
Imposing sets are best thing in this
absurd epic. Taylor plays great ruler
as if she's auditioning for a video
vixen while Burton portrays Mark
Antony as bored skirtchaser. And of
course, Dr. Doolittle is Julius Caesar.

Dick Tracy
(1990) 105m PG
*Warren Beatty, Madonna
D: Warren Beatty*
Tens of millions were squandered
on this attempt to render real life as
comic book. Watch first 10 minutes
to grasp film's inane style, then fast
forward to Al Pacino's scenes as
frantic villain.

Heaven's Gate
(1981) 220m R
*Kris Kristofferson, Christopher
Walken
D: Michael Cimino*
Costly western reviled only because
its ambition exceeds its worth. Dull
principals slow epic to a trot, but
strong supporting cast redeem
much. Not as good as it might have
been, but not nearly as bad as you've
been led to believe.

Howard the Duck
(1986) 111m PG
*Lea Thompson, Jeffrey Jones
D: Willard Huyck*
Duck from outer space lands on
Earth, saves it from evil overlords
while romancing woman punk
rocker. Costly endeavor fails on all
counts, though children under five
seem drawn to the alien quacker.

I'll Do Anything
(1993) 115m PG-13
*Nick Nolte, Albert Brooks, Julie
Kavner
D: James L. Brooks*
The musical that wasn't. Testings
proved so disastrous that all the
songs intended for this Hollywood
satire were scrapped. That anything
resembling a story survives is
thanks to talented cast.

Last Action Hero
(1993) 131m PG-13
*Arnold Schwarzenegger
D: John McTiernan*
Exhilarating, multi-level film re-
portedly cost $80 million and looks
it. (Okay, we couldn't just list bad
ones in this category). Chock full of
great scenes, crammed with cheeky
cameos.

One from the Heart
(1982) 100m R
*Teri Garr, Frederic Forrest
D: Francis Ford Coppola*
More notable for sinking Coppola's

Zoetrope Studios than for cinematic context as a jaded couple seek romantic excitement in a fantasy Vegas.

Santa Claus: The Movie
(1985) 112m PG
Dudley Moore, John Lithgow
D: Jeannot Szwarc
Costly film with scope and vision of commercials found on independent television at three in the morning. Moore isn't convincing as elf.

And the winner is:

Ishtar

(1987) 107m PG-13

Warren Beatty, Dustin Hoffman

D: Elaine May

Many millions were squandered on this smug, astonishingly empty "comedy" about untalented singing duo involved in foreign intrigue. Suitable only for screening in Dr. Kevorkian's waiting room.

The Bonfire of the Vanities
(1990) 126m R
Tom Hanks, Bruce Willis
D: Brian De Palma
Noxiously tame rendering of Tom Wolfe's gritty high-life crime-and-courtroom novel. Everyone seems lost here. Incredibly, Willis is miscast in role that calls for him to be smug and obnoxious.

Convoy
(1978) 106m R
Kris Kristofferson, Ali MacGraw
D: Sam Peckinpah
Maverick trucker leads convoy to protest gasoline prices. Avoid anyone who claims to enjoy this one.

Exposed
(1983) 100m R
Nastassia Kinski, Rudolf Nureyev
D: James Toback
College student becomes fabulous model overnight, romances famous violinist who is pursuing terrorists responsible for his mother's death. Truly stupid storyline undone by appalling cast.

F.I.S.T.
(1978) 145m R
Sylvester Stallone, Rod Steiger
D: Norman Jewison
Epic about young trucker's rise to union leadership and consequent corruption. Turns on premise that hard guys would vote for Stallone, 'cause he's a hard guy. Right.

Give My Regards to Broad Street
(1984) 109m PG
Paul McCartney, Linda McCartney
D: Peter Webb
More proof that Paul is indeed dead. Rock star searches for stolen tapes. Given the level of the tunes, you'll wonder why anyone would steal them or why he wants them back.

The Group
(1966) 150m
Candice Bergen, Shirley Knight
D: Sidney Lumet
Band of Vassar grads try to cope with real world of lesbianism, adultery, and nervous breakdowns. This stuff is a lot more interesting in real life.

Hudson Hawk
(1991) 95m R
Bruce Willis, Danny Aiello
D: Michael Lehmann
Smirking master burglar (guess who?) leaves prison and is promptly recruited by bone-headed CIA. Big-budget action-comedy makes trip to dentist office look appealing.

If Ever I See You Again
(1978) 105m PG
Joseph Brooks, Shelley Hack
D: Joseph Brooks
Fellow who wrote *You Light Up My Life* is star/writer/director of this romance about two long-ago lovers who attempt to rekindle flame. You'll want to kindle film.

Yentl
(1983) 134m PG
Barbra Streisand, Mandy Patinkin
D: Barbra Streisand
Plot: adult-looking girl masquerades as boy to facilitate study of Talmud. Though it has its fans, this one's much worse than it sounds.

The Adventures of Ford Fairlane
(1990) 101m R
Andrew Dice Clay, Priscilla Presley
D: Renny Harlin
Jerky detective probes death of heavy metal singer, manages to intrigue several women despite offensive manner. Funny if you like Clay, even funnier if you don't.

Faster Pussycat! Kill Kill!
(1966) 83m
Tura Satana, Haji, Lori Williams
D: Russ Meyer
Trio of sexy go-go dancers into hot-rodding in California desert soon find themselves involved in crime. A wild, wild ride for all.

Glen or Glenda
(1953) 70m
Edward D. Wood, Jr., Bela Lugosi
D: Edward D. Wood, Jr.
Amazing quasi-documentary about fellow who likes to wear girlfriend's clothes. Sweater swap sequence is touching classic. Wood's is among most unique perspectives in American film.

The Lonely Lady
(1983) 93m R
Pia Zadora, Lloyd Bochner
D: Peter Sasdy
Plain Jane marries screenwriter, then shows her own promise as writer, whereupon she's target of sexual abuse from Hollywooders. Zadora perfect in delightfully preposterous drama. Bochner lively too.

The Other Side of Midnight
(1977) 160m R
Marie-France Pisier, John Beck
D: Charles Jarrott
French woman gets dumped by American G.I., uses sex to climb social ladder and, eventually, get revenge. You'll laugh, you'll cry, you'll think, "I can come up with better crap than this."

Plan 9 from Outer Space
(1956) 76m
Bela Lugosi, Tor Johnson
D: Edward D. Wood, Jr.
Undisputed classic of its kind, replete with lame special effects, stilted dialogue, and clumsy performers. Lots of fun, even if every jerk you've ever known has seen it and recommended it. Tell him or her about *Convoy*.

Rock 'n' Roll High School
(1979) 94m PG
The Ramones, P.J. Soles
D: Allan Arkush
Ramones diehard manages to meet band and bring them to her high school, where they rock out and inspire riot. Crammed with Ramones classics.

Sorority Babes in the Slimeball Bowl-a-Rama
(1987) 80m R
Linnea Quigley, Brinke Stevens
D: David DeCoteau
Game gals and dimwits do battle with grotesque creature at mall. Does Rhonda Shearer know about this one?

And the nominees are:

All That Jazz
(1979) 120m R
Roy Scheider, Jessica Lange
D: Bob Fosse
Brilliant director/choreographer resembling S&M beatnik lives on the edge (cigarettes & sex) before having a heart attack. This one has its supporters.

The Green Berets
(1968) 135m G
John Wayne, David Janssen
D: John Wayne
Asinine pro-war drama in which crack battle leader justifies American presence in Vietnam by getting troops killed for pacifist journalist. So stupid, the sun actually sets in the east.

Homeboy
(1988) 118m R
Mickey Rourke, Christopher
*   Walken*
D: Michael Seresin
Vanity production for aspiring boxer Rourke, who plays low-level middleweight who's big opportunity is jeopardized by corrupt manager. Take the eight count.

The Last Movie
(1971) 108m R
Dennis Hopper, Julie Adams
D: Dennis Hopper
Stuntman tries to go native after filming Passion Play western in Peru. Really confused affair which repeatedly finds star/writer/director Hopper dwelling on his own confusion. This is your movie, this is your movie on drugs.

One Trick Pony
(1980) 100m R
Paul Simon, Joan Hackett
D: Robert M. Young
Simon also scripted this ludicrous drama in which he plays a diminutive, inexplicably desirable pop star whose record company keeps him from really rocking out.

A Star Is Born
(1976) 140m R
Barbra Streisand, Kris
*   Kristofferson*
D: Frank Pierson
Ghastly rock version of old warhorse about up-and-coming singer's marriage to an over-the-hill, alcoholic singer. It's long, it's lousy. You may never stop vomiting.

Stardust Memories
(1980) 88m PG
Woody Allen, Charlotte Rampling
D: Woody Allen
Brilliant director resembling insect is besieged by worshipful fans at film tribute in his honor. Portrait of the artist as utterly self-absorbed twerp.

Under the Cherry Moon
(1986) 100m PG-13
Prince, Kristin Scott Thomas
D: Prince
Effeminate pop singer dressed like
cowboy version of Ethel Merman ex-
erts inexplicable appeal on French
Riviera c. 1940s.

And the winner is:

Without You I'm Nothing

(1990) 94m

Sandra Bernhard

D: John Boskovich

Four-star rendering of Bernhard's unique,
amazing song-and-dance comedy act in which
she harangues herself and alienates nearly
everyone. Strip-tease finale is extraordinary.

A ZED AND TWO NOUGHTS

(1988) 115m

*Eric Deacon, Brian Deacon, Andrea
Ferreol*

It sometimes seems that Greenaway's
artistic intention is to render ugliness
in as beautiful–and, often, as inexplicably–a manner as possible. That's certainly the case in this truly bizarre account of twin zoologists mourning
their wives' joint deaths by filming the
decay of animal corpses swiped from a
nearby zoo. There's also a legless, bed-
bound seductress and a woman who
lusts after zebras. Greenaway's world
is a unique and–for those so inclined–
fascinating one.

Other Greenaway Greats:

The Baby of Macon (1993)

The Belly of an Architect (1991)

Prospero's Books (1991)

The Cook, the Thief, His Wife, and
  Her Lover (1990)

Drowning by Numbers (1987)

The Draughtsman's Contract (1982)

Best Use of Numbers within a Title

One Million B.C.
(1940) 80m
Victor Mature, Carole Landis
D: Hal Roach, Hal Roach, Jr.
Cavemen fight dinosaurs and each other in final days before advent of cable.

1900
(1976) 255m R
Robert De Niro, Gerard Depardieu
D: Bernardo Bertolucci
Two friends divided by class see the rise of Communism. Donald Sutherland dominates as the ruthless Attila, head-butter of cats. De Niro smirks a lot.

1918
(1985) 89m
Matthew Broderick, Hallie Foote
D: Ken Harrison
Life changes in a small town when influenza strikes and WWI rages in Europe. Scripted by Hallie's dad Horton from his play.

1941
(1979) 120m PG
John Belushi, Dan Aykroyd
D: Steven Spielberg
Sprawling, madcap comedy about West Coast catastrophe after Japanese submarine is sighted. Excellent dogfight sequence. Paced hysterically. Underrated.

1969
(1989) 96m R
Kiefer Sutherland, Robert Downey, Jr., Winona Ryder
D: Ernest Thompson
Trio of friends feel the effects of Vietnam War. Maybe they need a fourth.

Nineteen Eighty Four
(1984) 117m R
John Hurt, Suzanna Hamilton
D: Michael Radford
Stellar rendering of Orwell classic. Hurt and Hamilton are particularly strong as lovers in bleak, cynical world.

1991: The Year Punk Broke
(1992) 95m
Sonic Youth, Nirvana, The Ramones
D: David Markey
Several outstanding rock bands crank out the tunes. Nirvana featured too.

2001: A Space Odyssey
(1968) 139m
Keir Dullea, Gary Lockwood
D: Stanley Kubrick
Classic mindbender in which boy meets bone, boy meets slab, boy meets computer, boy meets slab again, and giant embryo looms in space. Easy.

And the nominees are:

The Brothers Karamazov
(1958) 147m
*Yul Brynner, William Shatner,
   Richard Basehart*
D: *Richard Brooks*
Ludicrous casting turns Dostoyevsky's masterpiece of psychology into soap opera in bad clothes. A must only for fans of *Star Trek* and *Voyage to the Bottom of the Sea.*

Moby Dick
(1956) 116m
Gregory Peck, Orson Welles
D: *John Huston*
Near catatonic sea captain is obsessed with revenge upon great white whale. Bad casting here too. Welles plays preacher, not whale.

A Passage to India
(1984) 163m PG
Judy Davis, Victor Banerjee
D: *David Lean*
Forster's novel of clashing cultures is reduced to a courtroom drama. Strong cast, particularly Davis, saves this from trashbin.

Ragtime
(1981) 156m PG
*Howard E. Rollins, Jr., Mary
   Steenburgen*
D: *Milos Forman*
Long and complicated adaptation of E.L. Doctorow's even more complex book about middle class family passions and scandals in 1906 America. James Cagney's last film role.

Swann's Way
(1984) 110m R
Jeremy Irons, Ornella Muti
D: *Volker Schlondorff*
Second part of the first book of Proust's 7-volume masterpiece is handsomely filmed and acted, but whole portions only make sense if you're one of the 9 people who've actually read the 3000-page original.

Ulysses
(1955) 104m
Kirk Douglas, Anthony Quinn
D: *Mario Camerini*
Homer's epic about the returning hero is transformed into dull saga of glistening men in one-shoulder tops, skirts, and sporty sandals perfect for work, play, or just plain eye-gouging with cyclops.

Ulysses
(1967) 140m
Milo O'Shea, Sheila O'Sullivan
D: *Joseph Strick*
Joyce's epic about a day in the life of a dull Dubliner is rendered even duller here. A must for insomniacs.

Under the Volcano
(1984) 112m
*Albert Finney, Jacqueline Bisset,
   Anthony Andrews*
D: *John Huston*
Good cast, unobtrusive direction can't obscure fact that Lowrie's subjective rendering of alcoholic's

demise is unfilmable. Have a drink instead.

War and Peace
(1956) 208m
Henry Fonda, Audrey Hepburn
D: King Vidor
Tolstoy's epic of the Napoleonic Wars is reduced to stuffy, awkward costume drama. Delightfully bad casting of all principals.

And the winner is:

The Bible

(1966) 155m

George C. Scott, Richard Harris

D: John Huston

Key work in Western civilization undone by hackneyed effects, absurd dialogue. Director Huston, master of bad, mad adaptations strikes again.

Canada's Sweetheart: The Saga of Hal C. Banks
(1985) 115m
D: Donald Brittain
True story of Banks, who was hired by the Canadian government to break up a strike among the communist-led seaman's union, which put a stranglehold on Canadian commerce.

The Decline of the American Empire
(1986) 102m R
Dominique Michel, Dorothee Berryman
D: Denys Arcand
8 academics spend a weekend together, shedding their sophistication and engaging in intertwining sexual hijinks.

Family Viewing
(1987) 92m
David Hemblen, Aidan Tierney
D: Atom Egoyan
Surrealistic depiction of a TV-obsessed family, whose existence is a textbook of home sweet dysfunctional home.

The Outside Chance of Maximillian Glick
(1988) 94m G
Noam Zylberman, Fairuza Balk
D: Allen E. Goldstein
Sentimental comedy about a boy's dreams and his tradition-bound Jewish family.

Roadkill
(1989) 85m
Valerie Buhagiar, Don McKellar
D: Bruce McDonald
Concert promoter tries to find lost band in the Canadian north woods. Along the way she meets a would-be serial killer and other assorted weirdos.

H
(1990) 93m
Martin Neufeld, Pascale Montpetit
D: Darrell Wasyk
Examines the lives of 2 junkies as they attempt to kick their heroin addiction. Includes explicit footage.

The Adjuster
(1991) 102m R
Elias Koteas, Arsinee Khanjian
D: Atom Egoyan
Insurance adjuster gets too caught up in his clients' problems, adversely affecting his own marriage.

Exotica
(1994) 104m
Bruce Greenwood, Mia Kirschner
D: Atom Egoyan
Troubled tax inspector becomes obsessed with young stripper at exotic club. Many secrets and side stories make for an uneasy multilayered saga.

The Tall Guy
(1989) 92m R
Jeff Goldblum, Emma Thompson
D: Peter Brewis
Loopy comedy in which bumbling American actor loses job in third-rate vaudeville show but lands title role in *Elephant Man* musical. Includes one of the all-time great furniture-displacing sex scenes.

The Unbelievable Truth
(1990) 100m R
Adrienne Shelly, Robert Burke
D: Hal Hartley
Aspiring model obsessed with Armageddon meets mysterious fellow who's returned home after serving prison sentence. Quirky comedy, with consistently unlikely dialogue; shot in a mere two weeks.

Dogfight
(1991) 94m R
River Phoenix, Lili Taylor
D: Nancy Savoca
Marine buddies compete to bring ugliest girl to party before departing for Vietnam in 1963. Poignant, off-beat fare.

Bad Lieutenant
(1992) 98m NC-17
Harvey Keitel
D: Abel Ferrara
Grim, incredibly seedy pic about worldly, repulsive lawman who finally finds something to believe in. Which doesn't stop him from being despicable.

Gas Food Lodging
(1992) 100m R
Ione Skye, Fairuza Balk, Brooke Adams
D: Allison Anders
Two sisters and their middle-aged mother enjoy what life they can in desert trailer park. Anders' directorial debut.

Boxing Helena
(1993) 107m R
Julian Sands, Sherilyn Fenn
D: Jennifer Lynch
Surgeon shows his love for gleeful bitch by holding her hostage and, furthermore, severing her limbs. Can true love be far behind?

The Music of Chance
(1993) 98m R
James Spader, Mandy Patinkin
D: Philip Johnson
Gambler and drifter lose wager with nerds at isolated mansion and consequently required to construct brick wall around premises. Then weird things start happening.

Red Rock West
(1993) 98m R
Nicholas Cage, Dennis Hopper
D: John Dahl
Hard-luck hero just can't seem to leave town where treachery awaits him at every turn. Hopper delivers yet another stellar turn as a charismatic manipulator.

Careful
(1994) 100m
Kyle McCulloch, Sarah Neville
D: Guy Maddin
Incest and deceit are the norm in this isolated Alpine community where significant sounds can trigger avalanches. You've never seen anything like this one–guaranteed!

Girlfriends
(1978) 87m PG
Melanie Mayron, Anita Skinner
D: Claudia Weill
Bittersweet story of a young Jewish photographer trying to make it on her own.

Gal Young 'Un
(1979) 105m
Dana Preu, David Peck
D: Victor Nunez
Rich woman, living in Florida's backwoods, is courted by younger man using her to set up his moonshine business.

Heartland
(1981) 95m PG
Conchata Ferrell, Rip Torn
D: Richard Pearce
Without cliche look at a woman's life on the Wyoming frontier. Set in 1910.

Street Music
(1981) 88m
Elizabeth Daily, Larry Breeding
D: Jenny Bowen
San Francisco's Tenderloin district finds a group of elderly residents banding together to save the old hotel they live in.

Old Enough
(1984) 91m PG
Sarah Boyd, Rainbow Harvest
D: Marisa Silver
Rich kid-poor kid coming of age friendship/comedy.

Blood Simple
(1985) 96m R
John Getz, M. Emmet Walsh
D: Joel Coen
Deviate, imaginative, morbid morality tale about a sleazy P.I. hired to kill an adulterous wife.

Smooth Talk
(1985) 92m PG-13
Laura Dern, Treat Williams
D: Joyce Chopra
Flirtatious but sheltered teenager catches the eye of a smooth-talking but shady older man.

The Trouble with Dick
(1988) 86m R
Tom Villard, Susan Dey
D: Gary Walkow
Ambitious young science fiction writer's personal traumas begin to show up in his work.

Waiting for the Moon
(1987) 88m PG
Linda Hunt, Linda Bassett
D: Jill Godmillow
Hunt's a treat as Alice B. Toklas but this bio of Gertrude Stein is ponderous and frustrating.

Heat and Sunlight
(1987) 98m
Rob Nilsson, Consuelo Faust
D: Rob Nilsson
Unique improvisational, video-to-film technique highlights a photographer's obsessive love and jealousy.

True Love
(1989) 104m R
Ron Eldard, Annabella Sciorra
D: Nancy Savoca
Savage comedy follows the events leading up to a Bronx Italian wedding.

Chameleon Street
(1989) 95m R
Wendell B. Harris, Jr.
D: Wendell B. Harris, Jr.
Fact-based story of a Detroit man who successfully impersonated a Yale student, Time magazine reporter, surgeon, and lawyer.

Poison
(1991) 85m R
Edith Meeks, Larry Maxwell
D: Todd Haynes
Three tales of obsessive, fringe behavior, including the chilling story of a 7-year-old's murder of his father.

In the Soup
(1992) 93m R
Steve Buscemi, Seymour Cassel
D: Alexandre Rockwell
Naive NY filmmaker sells his script to a fast-talking would-be producer who tries numerous and humorous ways to raise film money.

Ruby in Paradise
(1993) 115m R
Ashley Judd, Todd Field
D: Victor Nunez
Young woman leaves dead-end life in Tennessee, moves to Panama City, Florida, and attempts to make it on her own.

What Happened Was...
(1994) 92m
Tom Noonan, Karen Sillas
D: Tom Noonan
Edgy character study of an uneasy first date between 2 lonely people whose conversations reveal wounded psyches.

American Heart
(1992) 114m R
Jeff Bridges, Edward Furlong
D: Martin Bell
Untrusting ex-con reluctantly takes on teenaged son whom he barely recalls. Tough, realistic work.

Between the Lines
(1977) 101m R
John Heard, Jeff Goldblum
D: Joan Micklin Silver
Appealing comedy about goings on at an independent newspaper. Entire cast shines, with Goldblum especially memorable as music critic.

Crossing Delancey
(1988) 97m PG
Amy Irving, Peter Riegert
D: Joan Micklin Silver
Jewish grandma plays matchmaker for unlikely couple. Quirky, original take on modern love. Rent this one to impress your woman, or to disappoint your man.

Eureka!
(1981) 130m R
Gene Hackman, Theresa Russell
D: Nicolas Roeg
Klondike miner strikes gold, becomes rich old man. He eventually runs afoul of blow-torch wielding thugs. Bizarre courtroom climax replete with bad lighting.

Fingers
(1978) 89m R
Harvey Keitel, Jim Brown
D: James Toback
Aspiring pianist works as debt collector for mob boss. Guess which occupation prompts most of the film's action.

Home Movies
(1979) 89m PG
Keith Gordon, Kirk Douglas
D: Brian DePalma
Callow youth tries to find himself. Douglas is riotous as egotistic film professor, Nancy Allen hot as party girl for hire.

Max, Mon Amour
(1986) 97m
Charlotte Rampling, Anthony Higgins
D: Nagisa Oshimna
British diplomat in Paris discovers his wife is having an affair with a chimpanzee, then agrees that they should live as a menage a trois. Hardly predictable fare.

The Shout
(1978) 88m R
John Hurt, Susannah York, Alan Bates
D: Jerzy Skolimowski
Philandering composer finds his life undone when his wife succumbs to a stranger who possesses a shout that causes devastation and death. Keep your voice down.

Smash Palace
(1982) 100m
Anna Jemison, Bruno Lawrence
D: Roger Donaldson
Temperamental husband's bullying and obsession with cars undermines stability of his marriage. Intense, disturbing drama.

►

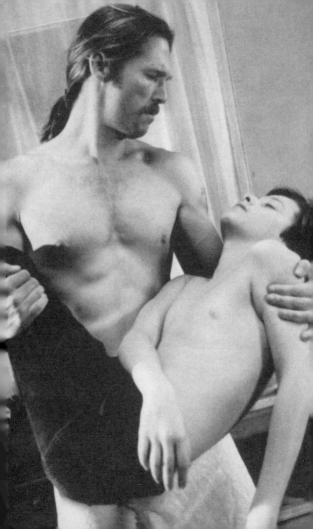

JE TU IL ELLE
(1974) 90m
Niels Arestrup, Claire Wauthion
D: Chantal Akerman

Akerman's is a strikingly varied cinema. She's made spirited musicals, threadbare documentaries, fragmented dramas, and harsh autobiographical works. Few filmmakers have bared their souls to greater effect than Akerman in *Je Tu Il Elle*, in which she assumes the principal role. Her character is a bored youth given to roaming nude through her bare apartment and consuming disturbing quantities of sugar. When she finally leaves her dull surroundings, she meets a good-natured trucker, whom she blandly provides with a sexual favor. She later turns up at the apartment of her female lover, with whom she is soon thrashing about in a long scene that renders lovemaking less a case of lust and more a bout of professional wrestling. The film is fun, disturbing, dull, preposterous, somewhat like life itself. See this, and demand that Akerman's masterpiece, *Jeanne Dielman*, be released on video too.

More Akerman:

Akermania, Volume 1 (1992)
Night and Day (1991)
Window Shopping (1986)
The Golden Eighties (1983)
Toute Une Nuit (1982)
Les Rendez-vous d'Anna (1978)
News from Home (1976)

Tess
(1980) 170m PG
Nastassia Kinski, Peter Firth
D: Roman Polanski
Engrossing adaptation of Thomas Hardy's *Tess of the D'Urbervilles*, as a poor girl struggles with love and class differences.

The Last Metro
(1981) 133m PG
Catherine Deneuve, Gerard Depardieu
D: Francois Truffaut
Actress tries to keep her Jewish husband's theatre going while she hides him from the Nazis and she falls for her leading man.

Three Men and a Cradle
(1986) 106m PG13
Roland Giraud, Andre Dussolier, Michel Boujenah
D: Coline Serrau
3 bachelors find themselves looking after the infant one of them fathered. U.S. remake: *Three Men and a Baby* (the French did it better).

Au Revoir, Les Enfants
(1988) 103m PG
Gaspard Manesse, Raphael Fejto
D: Louis Malle
Headmaster of Catholic boarding school tries to hide 3 Jewish boys from Nazis. Emotionally wrenching coming of ager.

Camille Claudel
(1989) 149m R
Isabelle Adjani, Gerard Depardieu
D: Bruno Nytten
Bio of young sculptress who falls for mentor Auguste Rodin, leading to madness and a orgiastic wallow in clay.

Too Beautiful for You
(1990) 91m R
Gerard Depardieu, Carole Bouquet
D: Betrand Blier
Man becomes overwhelmed by his beautiful wife and begins affair with frumpy secretary.

Cyrano de Bergerac
(1991) 138m PG
Gerard Depardieu, Anne Bochet
D: Jean-Paul Rappeneau
Grandly poetic adaptation of Edmond Rostand's drama about the noble poet/swordsman with an equally imposing nose.

All the Mornings of the World
(1992) 114m
Gerard Depardieu, Guillaume Depardieu
D: Alain Corneau
Depardieu pere and fils play 17th-century composer/cellist Marin Marais, examining his relationship with eccentric mentor Sainte Colombe.

Savage Nights
(1993) 126m
Cyril Collard, Romane Bohringer
D: Cyril Collard
Bisexual reacts to the news he has AIDS by not telling his 2 young lovers. Won best first film and best French film–a first.

The Lost Weekend
(1946) 100m
Ray Milland, Jane Wyman
D: Billy Wilder
Alcoholic can't believe he is one, experiences blackouts. Grim, unflinching depiction has lost little through time.

Wages of Fear
(1953) 138m
Yves Montand, Charles Vanel
D: Henri-Georges Clouzot
4 desperados in squalid Central American village agree to transport nitro through jungle in return for $2000 each. Bad judgement.

The Cranes Are Flying
(1958) 94m
Tatyana Samoilova, Alexei Batalov
D: Mikhail Kalatozov
WW2 heart-tugger finds a young man leaving his gal for the war. She winds up marrying his cousin.

La Dolce Vita
(1960) 175m
Marcello Mastroianni, Anita Ekberg
D: Federico Fellini
Tabloid reporter realizes the shallowness of his life in Rome society. One of Fellini's finest.

The Umbrellas of Cherbourg
(1964) 90m
Catherine Deneuve, Nino Castelnuovo
D: Jacques Demy
Bittersweet musical–completely free of spoken dialogue–about lovers who become separated by circumstance but are reunited years later.

Blow-Up
(1967) 111m
David Hemmings, Vanessa Redgrave
D: Michelangelo Antonioni
Swinging '60s London finds a photographer thinking his pictures reveal a murder in a park. Maybe it's too many drugs.

M*A*S*H
(1970) 116m R
Donald Sutherland, Elliott Gould
D: Robert Altman
Offbeat, highly entertaining black comedy about escapades of mobile surgical unit in Korean War. Numerous classic sequences, including unlikely football contest.

Taxi Driver
(1976) 113m R
Robert De Niro, Jodie Foster
D: Martin Scorsese
"You talkin' to me?!" New York City, a child prostitute, and a crazed (and mohawked) De Niro.

Apocalypse Now
(1979) 150m R
Marlon Brando, Martin Sheen
D: Francis Ford Coppola
Vietnam War epic paralleling Joseph Conrad's *Heart of Darkness*. Fraught with conflict (and egos)–somehow it all works out.

Man of Iron
(1981) 140m
Jerzy Radziwilowicz, Krystyna Janda
D: Andrzej Wajda
Filmmaker marries the son of the fallen worker/hero whose life she's

researching. Sequel to *Man of Marble*.

Paris, Texas
(1984) 145m PG
Harry Dean Stanton, Nastassia Kinski
D: Wim Wenders
Bleak barren drama about drifter's efforts to rekindle ties with son and find long gone wife in bleak, barren American southwest. Written by Sam Shepard.

When Father Was Away on Business
(1985) 135m R
Moreno D'E Bartolli, Miki Manojlovica
D: Emir Kusturica
6-year-old tries to understand what's happening to his family when his father is sent to a labor camp. Set in '50s Sarajevo.

The Mission
(1986) 125m PG
Robert De Niro, Jeremy Irons
D: Roland Joffe
Jesuit mission in 18th-century Brazilian jungle is threatened by greed and politics. Odd casting; beautiful production.

Overseas: Three Women with Man Trouble
(1990) 96m
Nicole Garcia, Marianne Basler, Brigitte Rouan
D: Brigitte Rouan
Trio of attractive sisters must cope with emotional turmoil while living in colonial Algeria. Action is considered from each sister's perspective.

Sort of like *Rashomon* meets the Foreign Legion.

Wild at Heart
(1990) 125m R
Nicolas Cage, Laura Dern
D: David Lynch
Lusty couple find excitement and danger in bleak, barren American southwest. Not for everyone. Not written by Sam Shepard.

The Best Intentions
(1992) 182m
Samuel Froler, Pernilla August
D: Bille August
Sumptuous drama recounts arduous courtship and early marriage of screenwriter Ingmar Bergman's parents. Swedish gloom rendered in usual superlative fashion.

My New Gun
(1992) 99m R
Diane Lane, Stephen Collins
D: Stacy Cochran
Twisted comedy about suburban couple whose lives are undone when they obtain gun. James LeGros shines as peculiar neighbor. Film opened small and stayed that way.

Farewell My Concubine
(1993) 157m R
Leslie Cheung, Zhang Fengyi, Gong Li
D: Chen Kaige
Epic melodrama about bond between two stars of Peking Opera. Li is particularly strong in supporting role.

The Bicycle Thief
(1948) 90m
Lamberto Maggiorani, Lianella Carell
D: Vittorio De Sica
Classic tale of worker's efforts to recover stolen bicycle. Ranks among greatest films ever made.

Black Orpheus
(1958) 103m
Breno Mello, Marpessa Dawn
D: Marcel Camus
Orpheus legend transplanted to Brazil during the carnival. Among cinema's most underrated works.

8 1/2
(1963) 135m
Marcello Mastroianni, Claudia Cardinale
D: Federico Fellini
Account of filmmaker's block, with the hapless filmmaker besieged by well-meaning friends and acquaintances at a spa. No plot synopsis does justice to this unique masterwork.

Get Out Your Handkerchiefs
(1978) 109m
Gerard Depardieu, Patrick Dewaere, Carole Laure
D: Bertrand Blier
Hapless husband pairs his unfulfilled wife with a stranger. The men become friends and the wife withdraws even further. Unlikely and unforgettable comedy.

La Strada
(1954) 107m
Giulietta Masina, Anthony Quinn
D: Federico Fellini
Affectionate, somewhat simple-minded clown is abused by her brutish strongman husband. Memorable, if sobering, drama.

Pelle the Conqueror
(1988) 160m
Pelle Hvenegaard, Max von Sydow
D: Bille August
Father and son find work for a landowner in late 19th-century Denmark. Hardships abound but the duo remain close. The son, though, aspires to see world beyond field.

Rashomon
(1951) 83m
Toshiro Mifune, Masayuki Mori
D: Akira Kurosawa
Husband and wife traveling through woods are attacked by a bandit. Unique examination of truth as different characters recall same event but describe quite different actions.

Through a Glass Darkly
(1961) 91m
Harriet Andersson, Max von Sydow
D: Ingmar Bergman
In isolation, a woman goes mad to the chagrin of those around her. Quintessential Bergman.

► *La Strada (1954)*

And the nominees are:

First Name: Carmen
(1984) 85m
*Maruschka Detmers, Jacques
   Bonnaffe*
D: Jean-Luc Godard
Security guard becomes sexually
obsessed with attractive bank robber. She's more concerned with
raising funds for her loony uncle's
film project.

The Home and the World
(1984) 130m
*Victor Banerjee, Soumitra
   Chatterjee*
D: Satyajit Ray
Young woman becomes drawn to
her steadfast husband's charismat-
ic, reckless activist friend.

La Notte
(1961) 120m
*Jeanne Moreau, Marcello
   Mastroianni*
D: Michelangelo Antonioni
Married couple endure alienation
from each other, fornicate on estate
lawn. Antonioni in his element.

The Moon in the Gutter
(1983) 109m R
*Gerard Depardieu, Nastassia
   Kinski*
D: Jean-Jacques Beineix
While searching for his sister's
murderer, dockworker is drawn to
fetching socialite, even though he

already has hot item at home. Stylized masterwork.

My Twentieth Century
(1990) 104m
Dorotha Segda, Oleg Jankowski
D: Ildiko Enyedi
Twins are separated as children.
One becomes a political radical, the
other, a seductress. Eventually their
paths cross.

Time of the Gypsies
(1990) 136m R
*Davor Dujmovic, Sinolicka
   Trpkova*
D: Emir Kusturica
Gripping account of young gypsy's
loss of innocence in world of crime
and exploitation. Not for the faint of
heart.

Under Satan's Sun
(1987) 97m
*Gerard Depardieu, Sandrine
   Bonnaire*
D: Maurice Pialat
Masochistic priest discovers he may
actually be capable of miracles, but
doesn't feel better for it. Maybe the
hairshirt isn't tight enough.

Wedding in Blood
(1974) 98m PG
Claude Pieplu, Stephane Audran
D: Claude Chabrol
Married lovers plot to eliminate

their respective mates. Typical
Chabrol study of smug fools.

And the winner is:

Two English Girls

(1972) 132m R

*Kika Markham, Stacey Tendeter, Jean-Pierre
Leaud*

D: Francois Truffaut

A complement to Trufaut's *Jules and Jim* (1961),
this dark romantic triangle features Leaud as an
aspiring writer at the beginning of the 20th-cen-
tury who enjoys strong ties to a pair of English
sisters. Based on a novel by Henri Pierre Roche
(also the author of *Jules and Jim*), with superb
cinematography by Nestor Almendros. Among
Truffaut's best.

Laughter Is a Universal Language Award– Best of the Foreign Funnies

Barjo
(1993) 85m
Anne Brochet, Hippolyte Giradot, Richard Bohringer
D: Jerome Boivin
Mentally unbalanced housewife tries to conduct affair with neighbor while hosting severely unbalanced brother, who chronicles her every move when not dwelling on extraterrestrial life.

Boyfriends and Girlfriends
(1988) 102m PG
Emmanuelle Chaulet, Sophie Renoir
D: Eric Rohmer
Girlfriends hit the mall, consider romantic options. Typical talky fare from France's eternally youngest, yet wisest, filmmaker.

The Funeral
(1984) 112m
Tsutomu Yamazaki, Nobuko Miyamoto
D: Juzo Itami
Japanese customs rarely appear more ludicrous than they do in this freewheeling work about a family's funeral preparations.

Leningrad Cowboys Go America
(1989) 78m PG-13
Matti Pellonpaa, Kari Vaananen
D: Aki Kaurismaki
Inexcusably lame Euro-rockabilly band find something less than widespread fame in the states. But they have incredibly cool haircuts, with shoes that match.

Men
(1985) 96m
Heiner Lauterbach, Uwe Ochsenknecht
D: Doris Dorrie
Businessman discovers his wife is having an affair with young artist. As revenge, he befriends the Bohemian and changes him into white-collar stiff.

Smiles of a Summer Night
(1955) 110m
Harriet Andersson, Gunnar Bjornstrand
D: Ingmar Bergman
Sexual shenanigans of a high order ensue when various couples plot to alter pairings. Of course, this is Bergman, so there is a suicide attempt. But it turns out to be the single funniest scene.

Sugarbaby
(1985) 103m R
Marianne Sagebrecht, Eisi Gulp
D: Percy Adlon
Fat woman turns seductive to win love of handsome subway conductor. Relax, it's a comedy.

Women on the Verge of a Nervous Breakdown
(1988) 88m R
Carmen Maura, Antonio Banderas
D: Pedro Almodovar
Comedy of errors in which bad timing, bad feelings, and a batch of spiked gazpacho subvert the plans of several wacky folks. Somewhat tame Almodovar still provides plenty of laughs.

78

College
(1927) 60m
Buster Keaton
D: James W. Horne
Hapless hero auditions for various collegiate sports. Features convenient use of pole vault.

The Gold Rush
(1925) 85m
Charlie Chaplin
D: Charlie Chaplin
Superior mirthmaker includes riotous dining scene in which starved miner imagines the Tramp as a meal while Tramp himself eats shoelace as if it were tasty noodle.

The General
(1927) 78m
Buster Keaton
D: Buster Keaton, Clyde Bruckman
Indefatigable Buster fights for Rebs during the Civil War. Stunning train sequence never fails to spark laughs.

The Italian Straw Hat
(1927) 72m
Albert Prejean
D: Rene Clair
Chain of errors ensues when a man attempts to replace a woman's hat that's been consumed by his horse.

Modern Times
(1936) 87m
Charlie Chaplin
D: Charlie Chaplin
The tramp falls victim to a machine, proffers cocaine, and executes deft roller-skating maneuvers. Chaplin's masterpiece.

Safety Last
(1923) 78m
Harold Lloyd
D: Fred Newmeyer
This is the one where the hero hangs from the hand of a clock looming over a busy downtown. Lloyd did his own stunts. (Take that, Arnold.)

Silent Movie
(1976) 88m PG
Mel Brooks, Marty Feldman
D: Mel Brooks
Destitute filmmaker tries to revive career and salvage his Miracle Studios. "If it's a good picture, it must be a Miracle."

Steamboat Bill, Jr.
(1928) 75m
Buster Keaton
D: Charles Reisner
This is the one where the hero survives a cyclone even after a house is blown onto him. No one has ever been more fascinatingly funny than Keaton.

The Awful Truth

(1937) 92m
Cary Grant, Irene Dunne
D: *Leo McCarey*

Screwball masterpiece in which married couple embark on separate lives only to discover that, after all, they are made for each other.

Born Yesterday

(1950) 103m
Judy Holiday, William Holden
D: *George Cukor*

Brutish gangster decides his tootsie needs educating and hires attractive fellow as teacher. Jeez, you think the gal and the teacher fall in love?

Casanova's Big Night

(1954) 85m
Bob Hope, Joan Fontaine
D: *Norman Z. McLeod*

Incredible coward poses as dashing Casanova and soon runs afoul of rogues in backlot Venice. Hope's gift for evoking laughter here is indisputable.

It Happened One Night

(1934) 105m
Clark Gable, Claudette Colbert
D: *Frank Capra*

Sensational comedy that forever altered humankind's approach to hitchhiking. Sleeping scene is a classic too.

Love and Death

(1975) 89m PG
Woody Allen, Diane Keaton
D: *Woody Allen*

Gleeful coward inadvertently becomes hero in Napoleonic wars and then vows to kill Napoleon. His efforts are undermined rather severely.

A Night at the Opera

(1935) 92m
The Marx Brothers
D: *Sam Wood*

The Marx Brothers run amuck at opera house, rendering *Il Travatore* unfathomable. Boatroom scene is among all-time greats.

The Producers

(1968) 90m
Zero Mostel, Gene Wilder
D: *Mel Brooks*

Con men attempt to stage a Broadway flop only to find they have a hit. Timeless laugher includes notable *Springtime for Hitler* musical sequence.

Sabrina

(1954) 113m
Audrey Hepburn, William Holden, Humphrey Bogart
D: *Billy Wilder*

Two brothers compete for a fetching damsel's charms. Three leads all show considerable comedic flair.

Sullivan's Travels

(1941) 90m
Joel McCrea, Veronica Lake
D: *Preston Sturges*

One of Hollywood's greatest concerns an ambitious filmmaker who poses as a bum to obtain experience for making a serious, important film about life.

▶

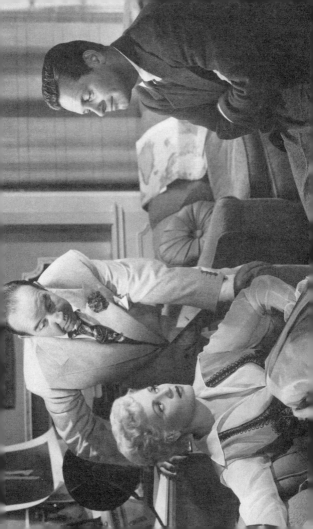

ZELIG

(1983) 79m PG
Woody Allen, Mia Farrow
D: Woody Allen

And sayeth the film encyclopedia, *Zelig* begot *Forest Gump*. Film-maker Allen has never been more stylistically radical than in this pseudo-documentary spanning the first half of the 20th-century. Leonard Zelig is an extraordinary individual capable of assuming the shape and behavior of anyone near him. This results in some riotous ethical alterations allowing Allen the actor to deliver some striking comic turns. But Allen the director, the dominant personality in Woody's ensemble, is most discernable here. The entire film is comprised of either authentic–or pseudo-authentic–footage, much of which nonetheless features Zelig. What a surprising technological age we live in! Zelig makes spring training with Lou Gehrig, and circulates with Charlie Chaplin and Douglas Fairbanks at a William Randolph Hearst bash. Testimonial footage abounds with such notables as Susan Sontag and Saul Bellow. Allen's never made another one like this, but techno whiz-kid Robert Zemeckis did.

Slightly Similar:

...And God Spoke (1994)
Fear of a Black Hat (1994)
Bob Roberts (1992)
Man Bites Dog (1991)
This Is Spinal Tap (1984)
Real Life (1979)

Aladdin
(1992) 90m G
D: Ron Clements, John Musker
Robin Williams' improvisational genius as the Genie threatens to overwhelm even Disney's stalwart animators in this adaptation of Arabian legends.

Allegro non Troppo
(1976) 75m PG
D: Bruno Bozzetto
Fantasia goes to Italy. More music, more wacky hijinx with animals.

Bugs and Daffy: The Wartime Cartoons
(1945) 120m
D: Robert McKimson, Chuck Jones, Friz Freleng
Funny, if somewhat disturbing, collection of propaganda toons. The Gremlin is great.

The Bugs Bunny/Road Runner Movie
(1979) 98m G
D: Chuck Jones, Phil Monroe
Best of Warner's collection that builds to extraordinary finale of Road Runner's greatest hits. Where is that Acme store anyway?

Dumbo
(1941) 63m
D: Ben Sharpsteen
Adorable elephant uses big ears to fly, buzzes circus tent. You'll need more than an umbrella after this one eats.

Fantasia
(1940) 116m
Plenty of fun for everyone as Mickey Mouse meets Carnegie Hall. Sequences range from the hallucinatory to the hilarious to the harrowing.

Fritz the Cat
(1972) 77m
D: Ralph Bakshi
It's as if Scorsese tried to make a kids' film. Funny, bawdy entertainment *for adults*.

Pinocchio
(1940) 87m G
D: Ben Sharpsteen
Adorable puppet uses big nose as lie detector, turns into donkey, gets swallowed by whale. Maybe he should go into politics.

Snow White and the Seven Dwarfs
(1937) 83m G
D: David Hand
Virgin finds refuge in woods with 7 malformed loners seeking gold. Sleep tight.

And the nominees are:

Blue Collar
(1978) 114m R
Richard Pryor, Harvey Keitel
D: Paul Schrader
Vivid drama of racism and working-class plight highlighted by stellar performance from Pryor.

The Color Purple
(1985) 154m PG-13
Whoopi Goldberg, Danny Glover
D: Steven Spielberg
South is setting for gripping drama about poor black woman in marriage to brute. Goldberg's best performance.

Dead Poets Society
(1989) 128m PG
Robin Williams, Ethan Hawke,
*   Robert Sean Leonard*
D: Peter Weir
Prep-school boys flourish under influence of charismatic English teacher who has problems with establishment. Stellar play from entire cast.

Driving Miss Daisy
(1989) 99m PG
Dan Aykroyd, Jessica Tandy,
*   Morgan Freeman*
D: Bruce Beresford
Aykroyd offers fine support as the concerned son of an aging southern matriarch, who comes to rely on her black chauffeur.

The King of Comedy
(1982) 101m PG
Robert De Niro, Sandra Bernhard
D: Martin Scorsese
Deluded comic and hyper henchwoman abduct beleaguered talk-show host (Jerry Lewis who's surprisingly sympathetic).

Leap of Faith
(1992) 110m PG-13
Steve Martin, Debra Winger
D: Richard Pearce
Evangelist con artist becomes stranded in farming community and befriends waitress. Martin's flamboyant minister calls to mind his early frantic comedy routines.

Mr. Saturday Night
(1992) 118m R
Billy Crystal, David Paymer
D: Billy Crystal
Tragedy about self-destructive comedian, Buddy Young, Jr., whose career span 5 decades while he alienates all around him. Paymer excels as his ever-patient brother.

The Razor's Edge
(1984) 129m PG-13
Bill Murray, Catherine Hicks
D: John Byrum
War veteran forsakes easy life and searches for spiritual meaning. Murray sincere in demanding role.

Tchao Pantin
(1984) 100m
Coluche, Richard Anconina
D: Claude Berri
Coluche, beloved French comic, succeeds against type as down-and-out ex-cop who befriends youth involved with drug dealers. Gloomy but compelling.

And the winner is:

Seize the Day

(1986) 93m

Robin Williams, Joseph Wiseman

D: Fielder Cook

Williams is gripping as manic, middle-aged failure desperate to realize business success and gain father's love. Adapted from novel by Saul Bellow, who appears in hallway scene.

OPENING NIGHT

(1977) 144m PG-13
John Cassavetes, Ben Gazzara
D: John Cassavetes

Few actresses come off tougher on screen than Rowlands, though in her best roles she inevitably conveys a sensitivity beneath that thick exterior. In her best film, Rowlands reverses herself, showing that determination exists beneath her scattered, vulnerable appearance. Here she plays an actress in out-of-town tryouts for a Broadway-bound drama. While shaping her role, Rowland's actress must contend with personal problems (romances with both her co-star and her manager), artistic problems (she's ill at ease in the role), and a peculiar tragedy involving the death of a fan. The entire film is fascinating, and Rowlands is a particularly good reason for seeing it.

More Rowlands:

Crazy in Love (1992)

Night on Earth (1991)

Once Around (1991)

Montana (1990)

Another Woman (1988)

An Early Frost (1985)

The Tempest (1982)

Gloria (1980)

A Woman Under the Influence (1974)

THE KILLING OF A CHINESE BOOKIE

(1976) 109m R

Ben Gazarra, Zizi Johari, Soto Joe Hugh

Cassavetes, who is probably best remembered as an actor with disturbing presence, made films of stark realism. His scenes unfold like portions of documentaries, and the dialogue sounds realistic instead of merely dramatic. In *The Killing of a Chinese Bookie*, a strip-joint operator runs up sizeable debts with a loan shark. When he can't pay the cash immediately, the loan shark offers him an alternative: Kill a local bookie. Although the hero suffers under the moral implications of the act, it actually seems simple enough to accomplish. But the targeted bookie is actually tied to Asian mobsters, and what starts out as a simple murder soon degenerates into a considerable problem. Be forewarned: Cassavetes's films are full of unsettling tension, bearing resemblance to Martin Scorsese's works. They are, thus, not for everyone.

Director John:

Love Streams (1984)

Gloria (1980)

Opening Night (1977)

Mikey & Nicky (1976)

A Woman Under the Influence (1974)

Husbands (1970)

Faces (1968)

Actor John:

Marvin & Tige (1984)

Whose Life Is It Anyway? (1981)

Brass Targets (1978)

The Fury (1978)

Rosemary's Baby (1968)

The Dirty Dozen (1967)

The Killers (1964)

Dark Victory

(1939) 106m

Bette Davis, George Brent, Humphrey Bogart

D: Edmund Goulding

Socialite is truly understood only by her masculine stable master (Bogart). Incurable disease steers this one away from absurdity and into fulfilling sadness.

Death in Venice

(1971) 124m PG

Dirk Bogarde, Bjorn Andresen

D: Luchino Visconti

Somber affair that starts slowly and proceeds into pathos punctuated occasionally by inappropriate flashbacks. Gloom, the lagoons, and the adagio from Mahler's 5th symphony–despair anyone?

The Fire Within

(1964) 104m

Maurice Ronet, Jeanne Moreau

D: Louis Malle

Emotionally withered hero overcomes alcoholism only to realize the true emptiness of life. After such an insight, can suicide seem a less than plausible act?

Hour of the Wolf

(1968) 89m

Liv Ullmann, Max von Sydow

D: Ingmar Bergman

Deranged artist is abused by his parasitic neighbors on a remote island. He's eventually attacked by a bird, whereupon his wife, one suspects, begins going mad too.

Long Day's Journey Into Night

(1962) 174m

Ralph Richardson, Katharine Hepburn, Dean Stockwell

D: Sidney Lumet

Each member of deluded family wrestles with an overwhelming weakness. Hepburn shines as a drug addict and Stockwell is equally memorable as tubercular youth.

Shame

(1968) 103m

Liv Ullman, Max von Sydow

D: Ingmar Bergman

Husband and wife survive during wartime only to find that their relationship is as bad as the war itself. Bergman's masterpiece, with a finale unequaled for relentless hopelessness.

Sophie's Choice

(1982) 157m R

Meryl Streep, Kevin Kline, Peter MacNicol

D: Alan J. Pakula

Aspiring writer plans his career and befriends a plucky Polish woman whose lover is gravely deranged. This is the comedy relief. The truly gruesome aspects involve the Holocaust.

Suddenly, Last Summer

(1959) 114m

Elizabeth Taylor, Montgomery Clift

D: Joseph L. Mankiewicz

Loopy drama in which valiant psychoanalyst tries to restore haunted socialite to sanity. It seems she has a rather bad memory: Her loving cousin, while vacationing, was killed and consumed by vicious street urchins.

SHORT CUTS

(1993) 189m R
Tim Robbins, Andie MacDowell, Jack Lemmon
D: Robert Altman

Altman found a kindred spirit in Raymond Carver, whose short stories provide all but one of the various narratives entwined here. It's life as usual on the West Coast, which means that all manner of peculiar events are taking place. And *Short Cuts* runs the gamut from comedy to drama. One couple contends with their son's state following a hit-and-run accident; the driver of that accident tries to deal with her dull life and her constantly inebriated lover; that lover, in turn, hits on the driver's daughter; and so it goes. A great deal is delivered here, with superb performances to boot. MacDowell, in particular, shines as the mother of the hospitalized boy. But Robbins, as an obnoxious motorcycle cop, is delightful in a comic turn, and both Lemmon and Anne Archer impress in more complex roles. One of Altman's best.

Variations:

Crooklyn (1994)
Reality Bites (1994)
Indian Summer (1993)
The Joy Luck Club (1993)
Menace II Society (1993)
American Heart (1992)
American Me (1992)
Peter's Friends (1992)
Boyz n the Hood (1991)
Grand Canyon (1991)
L.A. Story (1991)
Queens Logic (1991)
The Waterdance (1991)

City of Hope (1991)
Eating (1990)
Longtime Companion (1990)

Preludes:

Parenthood (1989)
St. Elmo's Fire (1985)
The Big Chill (1983)
Four Friends (1981)
The Four Seasons (1981)
Welcome to L.A. (1977)

Category: The Long Goodbye—Finest Deaths

And the nominees are:

Brian's Song
(1971) 74m G
James Caan, Billy Dee Williams
D: Buzz Kulik
True story of white pro footballer who befriends great black player, then gets cancer. A women's movie for men, or is it a men's movie for women? Keep the hankies handy. Kulik's masterpiece.

The Conformist
(1971) 108 R
Jean-Louis Trintignant, Dominque Sanda
D: Bernardo Bertolucci
Aloof fascist must prove worth by murdering former mentor. Culminating scene is truly disturbing in its realistic awkwardness.

Love Story
(1970) 100m PG
Ali MacGraw, Ryan O'Neal
D: Arthur Hiller
Future yuppie at Harvard meets poor music student. They marry, she gets protracted illness and dies, audience weeps, box office smiles. Bad 1978 sequel.

The Sheltering Sky
(1990) 139m R
Debra Winger, John Malkovich
D: Bernardo Bertolucci
American couple travel aimlessly through Sahara until hubby contracts horrible illness that renders him feverish and deranged. After he finally dies, his wife becomes sexual captive of desert sheik. Having a great time, wish you were here.

Some Came Running
(1958) 136m
Frank Sinatra, Shirley MacLaine
D: Vincente Minnelli
Writer returns to hometown, alienates family, befriends floozy who's being stalked. MacLaine's character gets it at amusement park. You'll wish everyone did.

The Stranger
(1945) 95m
Orson Welles, Loretta Young
D: Orson Welles
Nazi killer is discovered living in New England, gets brutal reminder that his time is up.

Terms of Endearment
(1983) 132m PG
Debra Winger, Shirley MacLaine, Jack Nicholson
D: James L. Brooks
Housewife betrayed by husband and harassed by obnoxious mother gets cancer. Winger takes forever to die, and it's kind of boring when she does. Don't bother with all this tearjerking, just fast forward to astronaut Jack's stuff.

90

Category: The Long Goodbye–Finest Deaths

Wild at Heart
(1990) 125m R
Nicolas Cage, Laura Dern
D: David Lynch

Runaway lovers encounter all manner of deranged folk, including Willem Dafoe's hypnotic geek, whose head gets sent into orbit.

And the winner is:

Ben-Hur

(1959) 212m

Charlton Heston, Stephen Boyd

D: William Wyler

Drama of Roman Empire Jew who gets betrayed by boyhood friend, becomes a slave, meets Jesus, becomes great charioteer, and meets ex-friend-turned-vicious-enemy in the arena. Since Boyd's the bad guy, guess who winds up getting knocked from his racing chariot, dragged around the racetrack, and trampled by horses?

91

HIGH TIDE
(1987) 120m PG-13
Jan Adele, Colin Friels
D: Gillian Armstrong

Davis has been typecast playing brittle, high-strung women in American films, thus some of her best work comes from abroad. *High Tide*, from Australian director Armstrong, is probably Davis's most impressive work. It's a steadily downbeat drama about a woman who loses her job–as backup singer to an Elvis impersonator–and finds herself in the trailer park where her daughter, abandoned long ago, now lives. Of course, mother and daughter meet again, and of course they develop an uneasy relationship. But its impossible to determine where the relationship is headed, or what Davis's character will ultimately do once her identity is discovered by her daughter. What is certain is that Davis, whether babbling a Bob Dylan song or performing an uneasy striptease, is a fascinating performer.

More Aussie Judy:

Georgia (1987)

Kangaroo (1986)

Heatwave (1983)

The Winter of Our Dreams (1982)

My Brilliant Career (1979)

Judy Elsewhere:

The Ref (1993)

Husbands and Wives (1992)

Alice (1990)

Judy in Costume:

Barton Fink (1991)

Naked Lunch (1991)

One Against the Wind (1991)

Where Angels Fear to Tread (1991)

Impromptu (1990)

A Passage to India (1984)

Breaker Morant
(1980) 107m PG
Edward Woodward, Bryan Brown, Jack Thompson
D: Bruce Beresford
Paths of Glory down under when 3 Aussie soldiers are tried for war crimes in the South African Boer conflict. Strong and disturbing, with great acting.

Gallipoli
(1981) 111m PG
Mel Gibson, Mark Lee
D: Peter Weir
Unforgettable WWI drama of 2 friends whose escapades lead them into the army and a bloody encounter with enemy Turks.

Careful, He Might Hear You
(1983) 113m PG
Nicholas Gledhill, Wendy Hughes
D: Carl Schultz
Boy becomes pawn in conflict between dead mother's sisters–one wealthy, one working-class–during Depression.

Bliss
(1985) 112m R
Barry Otto, Lynette Curran
D: Ray Lawrence
Outstanding surreal comedy about advertising executive who makes some disturbing discoveries after experiencing near-fatal heart attack.

Malcolm
(1986) 86m PG-13
Colin Friels, John Hargreaves
D: Naidia Tass
Twisted comedy about slightly retarded fellow who is drawn into criminal life. Similarities to American politicians are probably unintentional, certainly unavoidable.

The Year My Voice Broke
(1987) 103m PG-13
Noah Taylor, Loene Carmen
D: John Duigan
Teenage boy becomes infatuated with troubled girl. Downbeat, compelling.

The Navigator
(1988) 92m PG
Hamish McFarlane, Bruce Lyons
D: Vincent Ward
Boy in medieval England saves villagers from plague by conducting them through earth's core and into contemporary New Zealand, which is preferable.

Flirting
(1990) 100m R
Noah Taylor, Thandie Newton
D: John Duigan
Sensitive youth finds himself at odds with loutish peers, falls in love with girls-school outcast. Endearing drama is sequel to *The Year My Voice Broke.*

Proof
(1991) 90m R
Hugo Weaving, Genevieve Picot, Russell Crowe
D: Jocelyn Moorhouse
Cantankerous blind guy endures taunting, seductive housekeeper, befriends good-natured dishwasher, learns to trust (sort-of). Wonderfully wicked.

SWEETIE
(1989) 97m R
*Genevieve Lemon, Karen Colston,
Tom Lycos*

Most people who've wallowed in the
alleged romanticism of *The Piano*
would find it hard to believe that with
her first feature Campion won com-
parisons to John Waters and David
Lynch. This one's about an over-
weight sociopath who returns to family life and promptly unravels the
slight harmony that her parents and
sisters have achieved in her absence.
Her sister is rather deranged and already holds some unlikely phobias. Of
course, she becomes jealous when
Sweetie swaggers home, burned out record producer in tow, with
plans of becoming a recording star. The parents attempt to escape
but soon find themselves conducting Sweetie on a misbegotten vacation. Once back home, she suffers a mental breakdown and turns
up nude in a treehouse. But that's not all.

Offbeat Gems:

The Piano (1993)

An Angel at My Table (1990)

Films by Jane Campion [Passionless
   Moment, A Girl's Own Story,
   Peel] (1986)

Citizen Kane
(1941) 119m
Orson Welles, Joseph Cotton
D: Orson Welles
Millionaire newspaper magnate's stature declines in wake of sex-political scandal. Plotline only hints at film's power. It's a technical tour-de-force too.

Dr. Strangelove
(1964) 93m
Peter Sellers, George C. Scott
D: Stanley Kubrick
End-of-the-world comedy provides valuable insights into behind-the-scenes lunacy that seems to serve as standard operating procedure in world relations.

Goodfellas
(1990) 146m R
Ray Liotta, Robert De Niro
D: Martin Scorsese
Loopy, violent comedy-drama about mobsters. Friendships rarely last long in a ruthless world portrayed with frightening realism. Scorsese's best work.

The Graduate
(1967) 106m PG
Dustin Hoffman, Anne Bancroft,
Katherine Ross
D: Mike Nichols
College grad loves childhood friend but sleeps with friend's mother. Then things get ugly.

Network
(1976) 121m R
Faye Dunaway, Peter Finch
D: Sidney Lumet
We're still all mad as hell. Bleak comedy does to television communications what Strangelove does to diplomacy, as the whole world goes crazy.

The Piano
(1993) 120m R
Holly Hunter, Anna Paquin
D: Jane Campion
Girl loses voice–girl meets boy–girl loses piano–girl meets other boy–girl gets piano–other boy gets girl–boy gets mad–girl loses finger. Avoid people who find this film romantic.

Reds
(1981) 195m PG
Warren Beatty, Diane Keaton
D: Warren Beatty
Earnest communist tries to change America's ways, then gets sidetracked by Russian Revolution. When commie saga slows, fast forward to Jack Nicholson's scenes.

Stalag 17
(1953) 120m
William Holden, Otto Preminger
D: Billy Wilder
Aloof American becomes target of suspicion from fellow prisoners in German camp. Sometimes funny, sometimes frightening, always entertaining.

A Streetcar Named Desire
(1953) 122m PG
Marlon Brando, Vivien Leigh
D: Elia Kazan
Abuse-a-thon masterwork in which Southern belle fails to mix with her sister's loutish husband. Highlights include great argument about bowling.

And the nominees are:

Bill and Ted's Excellent Adventure
(1989) 105m PG
Keanu Reeves, Alex Winter
D: Stephen Herek
2 moronic youths encounter historic notables while time traveling as part of high school project, dude. Probably not fathomable by anyone over age 25.

48 Hours
(1982) 97m R
Eddie Murphy, Nick Nolte
D: Walter Hill
Seedy cop teams with streetwise convict to find killer drug lord. Rowdy, gleefully funny, but you might just want to fast forward to scenes where Murphy commands center stage.

Mean Streets
(1973) 112m R
Harvey Keitel, Robert De Niro
D: Martin Scorsese
Unlikely friendship between guilt-ridden Catholic and deranged punk bends but doesn't break in Little Italy crime world. Great soundtrack too.

Midnight Run
(1988) 125m R
Robert De Niro, Charles Grodin
D: Martin Brest
Bounty hunter and fugitive accountant bond while fleeing mobster and feds. "I just got two words to say to you: Shut the *&#- up.!"

Red Heat
(1988) 106m R
Arnold Schwarzenegger, Jim Belushi
D: Walter Hill
Cold-blooded Soviet cop joins with slob Chicago officer to capture vicious drug czar. Rowdy, grimly funny, but you might just want to fast forward to scenes where Arnold's lips move or his eyes glare.

Some Like It Hot
(1959) 120m
Tony Curtis, Jack Lemmon, Marilyn Monroe
D: Billy Wilder
Two musicians must disguise themselves as members of women's band to avoid recognition from gangsters. Somewhat dated, but still funny. Curtis fine mimicking Cary Grant.

Wayne's World
(1992) 93m PG-13
Mike Myers, Dana Carvey
D: Penelope Spheeris
Buffoonish youths find their public-access television show coveted by callous producer. What *Ishtar* was intended to be.

Withnail and I
(1987) 108m R
Richard E. Grant, Paul McGann
D: Bruce Robinson
Comedy about 2 unemployed actors compelled to shack up with flirtatious homosexual. It's from England.

And the winner is:

Thelma and Louise

(1991) 130m R

Susan Sarandon, Gena Davis

D: Ridley Scott

2 gals go on the lam after one of them blasts a would-be rapist. Their ensuing adventures repeatedly lead them to ignorant men, but then, that's true of anybody's adventures. Fun anyway. Harvey Keitel is actually sympathetic as the cop tracking the gals down.

Alice Doesn't Live Here Anymore
(1974) 105m PG
Ellen Burstyn, Kris Kristofferson
D: Martin Scorsese
Recent widow finds work in Phoenix diner and befriends kindly rancher. White bread Scorsese, but it's still better than what anyone else is serving.

Blazing Saddles
(1974) 90m R
Cleavon Little, Gene Wilder
D: Mel Brooks
Riotous comedy in which unlikely duo attempt to rid town of numerous villains and corrupt officials. Beans around the campfire make for a pleasant evening.

Chinatown
(1974) 131m R
Jack Nicholson, Faye Dunaway
D: Roman Polanski
Corruption aplenty in L.A., and that's the good news. Grotesque family secret is the bad news and detective Jack discovers that knowing about both doesn't help.

The Conversation
(1974) 113m PG
Gene Hackman, John Cazale
D: Francis Ford Coppola
Overlooked gem about eavesdropping specialist who realizes he may have uncovered a gruesome crime and that he might be in danger too. Paranoia strikes deep.

The Godfather II
(1974) 200m R
Al Pacino, Robert De Niro
D: Francis Ford Coppola
Sequel exceeds the original, with Michael Corleone imposing his coldblooded ways on the family business. Warmer flashbacks recount Papa Corleone's childhood and rise to power.

Harry and Tonto
(1974) 114m
Art Carney, Ellen Burstyn
D: Paul Mazursky
Quirky, warm-hearted comedy in which an old man and cat roam America, making new friends and renewing old acquaintances.

Lenny
(1974) 111m R
Dustin Hoffman, Valerie Perrine
D: Bob Fosse
Saga recounts comic Lenny Bruce's rise and fall, with numerous renderings of his own routines. Perrine's eye-opening strip is a Rewinders Classic.

Thieves Like Us
(1974) 123m R
Keith Carradine, Shelly Duvall
D: Robert Altman
Depression-era bank robbers become minor folk heroes despite relative incompetence. Crime story stripped of glamour and romance, but not drama.

The Three Musketeers
(1974) 105m PG
Richard Chamberlain, Raquel Welch
D: Richard Lester
Rowdy swashbuckler replete with twitching moustaches and heaving bosoms. And that's just Oliver Reed. Thoroughly entertaining.

▶

And the nominees are:

Child's Play
(1988) 95m R
Catherine Hicks, Alex Vincent
D: Tom Holland
Boy's toy doll is actually embodiment of deranged killer. Stupid adults, dorky kid, but really cool effects.

The Exorcist
(1973) 120m R
Linda Blair, Ellen Burstyn
D: William Friedkin
Demon-possessed girl begins spewing green projectile vomit, swears. Normal preadolescence? Her mother is perplexed. Bland priest has the answer.

Home Alone
(1990) 105m PG
Macaulay Culkin, Joe Pesci, Daniel Stern
D: Chris Columbus
7-year-old boy left behind by vacationing family lives high life while protecting home from two imbecilic thieves. Predictable fare salvaged by wild slapstick.

King of the Hill
(1993) 102m PG-13
Jesse Bradford, Jeroen Krabbe
D: Steven Soderberg
12-year-old must face life on his own, living in a seedy St. Louis hotel, while his father searches for work during the Depression. Based on memoirs by A.E. Hochner.

The Little Colonel
(1935) 80m
Shirley Temple, Lionel Barrymore
D: David Butler
Rebel disillusioned after Civil War has heart warmed again by incorrigible granddaughter. Temple is human equivalent of Pillsbury Doughboy.

Look Who's Talking
(1989) 90m PG-13
John Travolta, Kirstie Alley
D: David Kitay
Cynical baby provides running commentary while mother is courted by cabby. Bruce Willis shines in off-camera support.

My Girl
(1991) 102m PG
Anna Chlumsky, Macaulay Culkin
D: Howard Zieff
Preadolescent tomboy must come to terms with some of life's harsher realities.

National Velvet
(1944) 124m
Elizabeth Taylor, Mickey Rooney
D: Clarence Brown
Girl wins horse, decides to enter it in Grand National. Among best in girl-meets-horse genre.

Searching for Bobby Fisher
(1993) 111m PG
Joe Mantegna, Max Pomeranc
D: Steven Zaillian
7-year-old chess whiz perplexes parents, even when he's not kicking

keester on the Big Board. Based on true story.

The Slingshot
(1993) 102m R
Jesper Salen, Stellan Skarsgard
D: Ake Sandgren
12-year-old defies stodgy '20s Stockholm society thanks to enthusiastic inventiveness and determination.

And the winner is:

E.T.: The Extra-Terrestrial

(1982) 115m PG

Henry Thomas, Drew Barrymore

D: Steven Spielberg

Siblings life together escalates greatly in excitement after they befriend kindly, prune-fleshed alien. Popular pop fare.

Celeste
(1981) 107m
Eva Mattes, Jurgen Arndt
D: *Percy Adlon*
True story of dedicated maid and her employer, neurotic hypochondriac Marcel Proust.

Christiane F.
(1981) 130m R
Najta Brunkhorst, Thomas Haustein
D: *Ulrich Edel*
Young junkies party hard in Berlin. David Bowie appears in concert sequence.

Female Misbehavior
(1992) 80m
Camille Paglia, Annie Sprinkle
D: *Monica Treut*
Collection of films about women, including a pornographic actress and an S&M practitioner.

Kings of the Road
(1976) 176m
Rudiger Vogler, Hanns Zischler
D: *Wim Wenders*
Traveling film-projector repairman and friend roam West German countryside, have some fun. Wenders's finest work.

The Marriage of Maria Braun
(1979) 120m R
Hanna Schygulla, Klaus Lowitsch
D: *Rainer Werner Fassbinder*
Art-film melodrama about woman who compromises herself to remain true to her husband, who takes the rap when she murders her lover. You got all that?

The Nasty Girl
(1990) 93m PG-13
Lena Stolze
D: *Michael Verhoeven*
Student offends community while researching hometown's involvement with Nazis. Plus she swims naked.

Parsifal
(1982) 255m
Martin Sperr, Edith Clever
D: *Hans-Jurgen Syberberg*
Downright weird rendering of Wagner's musical sacrament. Landscapes include Wagner's nose, and at one point Parsifal turns into a woman. Oh well, the music's good.

Stroszek
(1977) 108m
Bruno S, Eva Mattes
D: *Werner Herzog*
Dim musician brings prostitute and old man with him to Wisconsin, the land of opportunity. They end up stealing a turkey.

The Tin Drum
(1979) 141m R
David Bennent, Angela Winkler
D: *Volker Schlondorff*
Boy refuses to grow beyond childhood height, raises a whole lot of hell in Nazi Germany.

A Woman in Flames
(1982) 106m R
Gudrun Landgrebe, Matthieu Carriere
D: *Robert Van Ackeren*
Bored housewife befriends male hustler, becomes S&M prostitute. Yeah, don't they all? Inspirational fare for unemployed.

AGUIRRE, THE WRATH OF GOD
(1972) 94m
Ruy Guerra
D: Werner Herzog

Kinski was a prolific, profligate performer who appeared in countless films. By his own estimation, only a few are worthwhile, with highest regard inevitably accorded to those directed by Herzog. A fanatical filmmaker, Herzog would appear to be Kinski's near-equal in temperament. Together the duo made 5 films, but they never made anything that surpassed *Aguirre, the Wrath of God*, an exhilarating, absurdist rendering on the Conquistadors. Kinski is awesome as a scheming officer who cunningly fosters rebellion and then foolishly maneuvers his troops into annihilation. It's lamentable that Kinski, an actor of impressive talent, chose to dictate his career in terms of quantity instead of quality, but it's fortunate that he linked with Herzog in creating a handful of stunning works.

Selected Kinski:

Crawlspace (1986)
Creature (1985)
His Name Was King (1985)
The Little Drummer Girl (1984)
Beauty and the Beast (1983)

Burden of Dreams (1982)
Fitzcarraldo (1982)
Woyzeck (1976)
Creature with the Blue Hand (1970)
Venus in Furs (1970)

Black Rain
(1989) 123m
Kazuo Kitamura, Yoshiko Tanaka
D: *Shohei Imamura*
Woman slowly dies after Hiroshima bombing. Meditative, moving.

The Cruel Story of Youth
(1960) 96m
Yusuke Kawazu, Miyuki Kuwano
D: *Nagisa Oshima*
Teenage girl and her geeky criminal boyfriend use sex to extort funds from rich businessmen. They probably become lobbyists.

Face of Another
(1966) 124m
Tatsuya Nakadai, Machiko Kyo
D: *Hiroshi Teshigahara*
Burn victim gets new face, turns into rapist-killer.

The Makioka Sisters
(1983) 140m
Keiko Kishi, Yoshiko Sakuma
D: *Kon Ichikawa*
Four sisters must be married off in between-the-wars Japan. A profound lament for the passing of a whole way of living.

The Seven Samurai
(1954) 204m
Toshiro Mifune, Takashi Shimura
D: *Akira Kurosawa*
Town of cowards recruits seven butt-kickin' soldiers to defend them against marauding bandits. Perhaps the greatest action movie ever made.

Tokyo Story
(1953) 134m
Chishu Ryu, Chieko Higashiyama, Setsuko Hara
D: *Yasujiro Ozu*
Masterpiece about aging husband and wife whose grown children see them as little more than a nuisance. Hara ranks among screen's most extraordinary presences.

Ugetsu
(1953) 96m
Machiko Kyo, Masayuki Mori
D: *Kenji Mizoguchi*
Clay worker becomes separated from community during wartime, falls in with beguiling ghost.

Vengeance Is Mine
(1979) 129m
Ken Ogata
D: *Shohei Imamura*
Psycho killer shows little sympathy for anyone. Intense exploration of evil.

When a Woman Ascends the Stairs
(1960) 110m
Hideko Takaamine, Tatsuya Nakadai, Masayuki Mori
D: *Miko Naruse*
Bar hostess must come to terms with aging (she's about to turn 30!) and finding an acceptable man.

THE LAST EMPEROR

(1987) 140m PG-13
John Lone, Joan Chen
D: Bernardo Bertolucci

Storaro has been described as a painter on film, and in this epic he provides some extraordinary imagery for director Bertolucci. A master at manipulating sunlight, Storaro infuses *The Last Emperor* with breathtaking hues and brilliant shades, particularly in the exterior shots of the Forbidden City. If Storaro is the closest that moviedom has to a painter, than the painter he most resembles is Vermeer, who also generated stunning work from the most simple light sources. But there's more to *The Last Emperor* than mere imagery, however stunning. It's a stirring chronicle of life–a rather comfortable life–in a void, and what happens when that void becomes a world of chaos. It won the Oscar for best film, but it's worth seeing anyway.

Best with Bertolucci:

Last Tango in Paris (1973)
1900 (1976)
The Sheltering Sky (1990)

Best of the Rest:

Apocalypse Now (1979)
Reds (1981)

105

Best of the Brits–The BAFTA Awards

The Lavender Hill Mob
(1951) 82m
Alec Guinness
D: Charles Crichton
Classic comedy has a timid bank clerk plotting an elaborate scheme to steal gold bullion. Watch with *The Man in the White Suit* for a double Guinness.

Richard III
(1955) 155m
Laurence Olivier, John Gielgud
D: Laurence Olivier
Shakespeare chronicle of twisted 15th-century British monarch and court intrigues.

The Bridge on the River Kwai
(1957) 161m
Alec Guinness, Sessue Hayakawa
D: David Lean
Blockbuster battle of wills between Japanese POW camp commander and British colonel. Escaped POW William Holden also gets involved.

Room at the Top
(1959) 118m
Laurence Harvey, Simone Signoret
D: Jack Clayton
Grim northern England setting finds ambitious young man sacrificing love to get ahead in business.

A Taste of Honey
(1961) 100m
Rita Tushingham, Robert Stephens
D: Tony Richardson
Plain girl has affair with black sailor and winds up pregnant. Poignant performances.

Lawrence of Arabia
(1962) 216m
Peter O'Toole, Omar Sharif
D: David Lean
Epic bio of British adventurer T.E. Lawrence and his support of the Arabs during WW1. Visual knock-out.

Tom Jones
(1963) 121m
Albert Finney, Susannah York
D: Tony Richardson
Engagingly bawdy adaptation of Henry Fielding's novel about an 18th-century playboy's adventures.

The Ipcress File
(1965) 108m
Michael Caine
D: Sidney J. Furie
Len Deighton thriller about cynical Cockney crook-turned-spy, Harry Palmer.

The Spy Who Came in from the Cold
(1965) 110m
Richard Burton, Claire Bloom
D: Martin Ritt
Embittered, aging Cold War spy (excellent work by Burton) comes to the end of his career. John Le Carre novel.

A Man for All Seasons
(1967) 120m
Paul Scofield, Robert Shaw
D: Fred Zinneman
Brilliant portrayals concern the 16th-century religious/political conflicts between English chancellor Sir Thomas More and King Henry VIII.

Sunday, Bloody Sunday
(1971) 110m R
Peter Finch, Glenda Jackson
D: John Schlesinger
Self-centered young man (Murray Head) is the object of desire for both Finch and Jackson. Adult fare.

The Elephant Man
(1980) 125m PG
John Hurt, Anthony Hopkins
D: David Lynch
Extremely malformed fellow alternately repels, charms withered Victorians. Outstanding turns from Hurt and Hopkins, surprisingly heartfelt perspective from Lynch.

Gandhi
(1982) 188m PG
Ben Kingsley, Edward Fox
D: Richard Attenborough
Conventionally rendered bio-epic about Indian leader who repelled occupying Brits through passive resistance. Kingsley is great.

Educating Rita
(1983) 110m PG
Julie Walters, Michael Caine
D: Lewis Gilbert
Brassy working-class woman decides to study literature, gains attention of charming, alcoholic tutor. Both leads shine.

A Room with a View
(1986) 117m
Helena Bonham Carter, Julian Sands
D: James Ivory
Sterling adaptation of E.M. Forster's funny, moving novel about woman who rejects dashing suitor for stuffy fiance (Daniel Day-Lewis). Excellent in every way.

Hope and Glory
(1987) 97m PG-13
Sebastian Rice Edwards, Sarah Miles
D: John Boorman
London WW2 bombings as seen from perspective of wide-eyed, adventurous boy. Funny, occasionally fantastic.

The Commitments
(1992) 116m R
Andrew Strong, Michael Aherne
D: Alan Parker
Working-class Dublin youths form soul band, sweating and swearing. Under the Shamrock Moon.

Shadowlands
(1994) 130m PG
Anthony Hopkins, Debra Winger
D: Richard Attenborough
True story of theologian C.S. Lewis's romance with American divorcee Joy Gresham. Earlier version, featuring Joss Ackland and Claire Bloom, is equally moving and 40 minutes shorter.

Margaret Thatcher Memorial Award: Best of British Television

And Now for Something Completely Different
(1972) 89m PG
Monty Python's Flying Circus
D: Ian McNaughton
Delightful collection of zany, original skits, including the Dead Parrot and the Lumberjack Song.

Brideshead Revisited
(1981) 540m
Jeremy Irons, Anthony Andrews
D: Charles Sturridge, Michael Lindsay-Hogg
Crowning achievement in British TV remains this tale of a young man's romantic involvement with an upper-crust family. Star turns all around.

I, Claudius
(1980) 708m
Derek Jacobi, Sian Phillips, John Hurt
D: Herbert Wise
Addictive take on Roman decadence, with enough intrigue and deceit for everyone. Hurt's deranged Caligula further enlivens already entertaining work.

Jane Eyre
(1983) 239m
Zelah Clarke, Timothy Dalton
D: Julian Aymes
Emily Bronte's classic about faithful Jane, masculine Rochester, and the mad woman in the attic is brought to the screen in copious detail.

The Jewel in the Crown
(1984) 750m
Charles Dance, Geraldine James
D: Christopher Morahan, Jim O'Brien
Epic tale of Brits in India during the final period of the Raj. Rape, rebellion, and a villain devoted to Sousa marches.

Poldark
(1975) 720m
Robin Ellis, Angharad Rees
D: Paul Annett, Christopher Barry
Dashing hero, feisty heroine, dastardly villain, forbidden love--all set in 18th-century Cornwall. Not great literature but lots of fun.

Pride and Prejudice
(1985) 226m
Elizabeth Garvie, David Rintoul
D: Cyril Coke
Stellar, if protracted, take on Jane Austen's masterpiece about true love and proper place settings. You can probably read the book in less time.

Prime Suspect
(1992) 240m
Helen Mirren, Tom Bell
D: Christopher Menaul
Top notch mystery/character study in which female office investigator must overcome office prejudice while tackling difficult sex-crime case. 2 compelling sequels.

CAL

(1984) 104m R

John Lynch

D: Pat O'Connor

In this drama about the Catholic-Protestant conflict in Northern Ireland, Mirren shines brightly as a middle-aged widow whose husband, a policeman, has been murdered by youthful members of the IRA. She befriends and falls in love with Cal, the shy, soft-spoken young man who served as the getaway driver for her husband's murderers. An actress of extraordinary range and subtle expression, Mirren has not always been properly utilized in films, where she frequently appears in supporting roles. *Cal*, which earned her Best Actress at the Cannes Film Festival, is evidence that she ranks with the most distinguished of her profession.

Intriguing Mirren:

Prime Suspect 3 (1994)

The Hawk (1993)

Prime Suspect 2 (1993)

Prime Suspect (1992)

The Comfort of Strangers (1991)

Where Angels Fear to Tread (1991)

Coming Through (1990)

The Cook, the Thief, His Wife & Her Lover (1990)

When the Whales Came (1989)

Pascali's Island (1988)

The Mosquito Coast (1986)

White Knights (1985)

Excalibur (1981)

The Long Good Friday (1979)

O Lucky Man (1973)

A Midsummer Night's Dream (1968)

ALTERED STATES

(1980) 103m R
William Hurt, Blair Brown
D: Ken Russell
Obsessed with uncovering the essence of life, a scientist sacrifices himself and the love of a good woman. He doesn't really lose either, though. He just wallows in a sensory-deprivation tank and endures some truly bizarre visions; then treks to the desert, takes a bloody drug, and endures some truly bizarre visions; then heads back to the tank where, of course, he temporarily turns into a ravenously-carnivorous primate. Eventually he evolves into some glowing thing out of 50s sci fi. Then his naked wife saves him. Okay, so you know what happens. See it anyway and vicariously destroy some brain cells. Paddy Chayefsky tried to screenwrite from his own novel before calling it quits and asking that his name be removed from the credits.

Head Trips:
The Doors (1991)
Until the End of the World (1991)
Koyaanisqatsi (1983)
Pink Floyd: The Wall (1982)
Tommy (1975)
Zacharia (1970)
2001: A Space Odyssey (1968)
Head (1968)
The Trip (1967)

THE LAIR OF THE WHITE WORM

(1988) 93m R

Amanda Donohoe, Sammi Davis-Voss, Hugh Grant

Usually, the weirder Russell is, the worse he is. Happily, that's not the case in this offbeat, strangely funny horror entry. It seems that some young people have run afoul of a sexy vampire who's come to Scotland to pay homage to a massive worm under an old farmhouse. This film's replete with bizarre hallucinations (a Russell trademark), a rule-breaking vampire who stalks about in the daytime, and, of course, the worm itself, which appears as a howling maggot eager to get at a sacrifice victim writhing in starched white underwear. Donohoe, as the vampire worm-worshipper, is the go-for-broke star here. She's sexy, funny, and scary, sometimes all at once. Highlights include Donohoe emerging from her tanning-booth coffin and another of her conducting a seduction that soon turns perilous for her partner.

Russell Unbound:

Whore (1991)

The Rainbow (1989)

Salome's last Dance (1988)

Gothic (1987)

Crimes of Passion (1984)

Altered States (1980)

Valentino (1977)

Lisztomania (1975)

Tommy (1975)

Mahler (1974)

The Music Lovers (1971)

The Devils (1971)

Women in Love (1970)

And the nominees are:

Bix
(1990) 100m
Bryant Weeks, Emile Levisetti
D: Pupi Avati
Flashback narrative recounts life of premier jazz cornetist Bix Beiderbecke, who died at age 28.

Coal Miner's Daughter
(1980) 125m PG
Sissy Spacek, Tommy Lee Jones
D: Michael Apted
Bio of country star Loretta Lynn. Spacek is perfect in lead, even does her own singing.

The Fabulous Baker Boys
(1989) 116m R
Jeff Bridges, Beau Bridges, Michelle Pfeiffer
D: Steven Kloves
Stability of brother pianists' lounge act is threatened when they take on a singer and Jeff falls for her. Notable vamping by Pfeiffer.

Lisztomania
(1975) 108m R
Roger Daltrey, Fiona Lewis
D: Ken Russell
Russell strikes again in this wild reflection on great pianist-composer Liszt. Who's lead singer Daltrey is spirited in lead, comely Lewis better as his lover in opening metronome sequence.

The Music Lovers
(1971) 122m R
Richard Chamberlain, Glenda Jackson
D: Ken Russell
Over-the-top bio of Tchaikovsky focuses on the homosexual composer's marriage to a nymphomaniac. Welcome to the world of Ken Russell.

Purple Rain
(1984) 113m R
Prince, Morris Day
D: Albert Magnoli
He whose name can no longer be pronounced made this long-form autobiographical music video at the peak of his career. Answers the question: can a black guy who wears heels and sings in the upper registers make it in Minneapolis?

Spring Symphony
(1986) 93m PG-13
Rolf Hoppe, Nastassia Kinski
D: Peter Schamoni
Romantic bio of Romantic composer Robert Schumann and his love for pianist Clara Weick. Fine soundtrack, as one might expect.

Sweet Dreams
(1985) 115m PG-13
Jessica Lange, Ed Harris
D: Karel Reisz
Bio of country star Patsy Cline focuses on her turbulent marriage as well as her extraordinary career.

Tender Mercies
(1983) 88m PG
Robert Duvall, Tess Harper
D: Bruce Beresford
Downtrodden drunk revives his life and his country-music career through love of a good woman. "Didn't you used to be Mac Sledge?"

And the winner is:

Round Midnight

(1986) 132m R

Dexter Gordon, Francois Cluzet

D: Bertrand Tavernier

Extraordinary account of drug-addict jazz saxophonist and his friendship with worshipful fan. Jazz great Gordon won Oscar nomination for truly moving performance.

Aladdin

(1992) 90m G
D: Ron Clements, John Musker
Animated rendering of kids' classic about boy with magic lamp and helpful genie. With music by Alan Menken, Howard Ashman, and Tim Rice.

Amadeus

(1984) 158m PG
F. Murray Abraham, Tom Hulce
D: Milos Forman
Well of course the score's great–we're talking Mozart! Even if Wolfgang A. is presented as a boyish, boorish genius.

Beauty and the Beast

(1991) 84m G
D: Kirk Wise, Gary Trousdale
Beloved–that is, extensively promoted–cartoon version of village girl's unlikely affection for monster. Tunes by Alan Menken and Howard Ashman.

Chariots of Fire

(1981) 123m PG
Ben Cross, Ian Charleson
D: Hugh Hudson
True story of 2 runners from Great Britain training for the Olympics of 1924. Memorable score from Vangelis.

The Crow

(1993) 100m R
Brandon Lee, Michael Wincott
D: Alex Proyas
Fantastic revenge drama in which murdered youth returns for payback on Devil's Night. Ominous music by Graeme Revell.

Dances with Wolves

(1990) 181m PG-13
Kevin Costner, Mary McDonnell
D: Kevin Costner
Army officer finds adventure and personal insights among Indians in American west. Sweeping score by masterful John Barry.

Dirty Dancing

(1987) 97m PG-13
Jennifer Grey, Patrick Swayze
D: Emile Ardolino
Fetching gal falls for hip cat in Catskills c. 1963. Score by John Morris.

Fame

(1980) 133m R
Irene Cara, Paul McCrane
D: Alan Parker
Moving account of 8 students at New York's High School of Performing Arts. Music by Michael Gore.

In the Name of the Father

(1993) 133m R
Daniel Day-Lewis, Peter Postlethwaite
D: Jim Sheridan
True story of Irish father and son wrongly imprisoned by English for IRA terrorism. With tunes from Bono and Sinead O'Connor.

The Last of the Mohicans

(1992) 114m R
Daniel Day-Lewis, Madeleine Stowe
D: Michael Mann
Soaring score by Trevor Jones and Randy Endelman complements action-packed adventure and gorgeous stars.

National Lampoon's Animal House

(1978) 109m R
John Belushi, Tim Matheson
D: John Landis
Wild comedy about wild fraternities in those wild early 60s. Includes concert sequence from Otis Day and the Knights. Other music by Elmer Bernstein.

Out of Africa

(1985) 161m PG
Meryl Streep, Robert Redford
D: Sydney Pollack
True story of Danish writer who falls in love with English adventurer while managing African coffee farm. Majestic music courtesy of John Barry.

Philadelphia

(1993) 125m PG-13
Tom Hanks, Denzel Washington
D: Jonathan Demme
Attorney loses job because of AIDS, so he sues former employers. His own attorney, by the way, is a homophobe. Somber tunes from Bruce Springsteen and Neil Young.

The Piano

(1993) 120m R
Holly Hunter, Harvey Keitel
D: Jane Campion
Mute gal marries dull land owner in New Zealand, then falls for tattooed settler who has bought her piano. Hunter herself plays Michael Nyman's keyboard scores.

Reality Bites

(1994) 99m PG-13
Winona Ryder, Ethan Hawke
D: Ben Stiller
Comedy concerns recent college grads hanging out in Houston. Tunes from a slew of alternative bands plus the Knack with "My Sharona."

Schindler's List

(1993) 195m R
Liam Neeson, Ralph Fiennes
D: Steven Spielberg
Stirring account of one man's efforts to save Jews during the Holocaust. Stirring score, too, courtesy of Speilberg staple John Williams.

Singles

(1992) 100m PG-13
Matt Dillon, Bridget Fonda
D: Cameron Crowe
Twentysomethings hang out in Seattle. Tunes from such greats as Pearl Jam, Alice in Chains, Soundgarden, and Mudhoney.

Somewhere in Time

(1980) 103m PG
Christopher Reeve, Jane Seymour
D: Jeannot Szwarc
Romantic John Barry score, romantic setting, suspend-your-brains romantic plot about modern playwright falling for 1912 beauty.

Unplugged Award–Best of Rock Stars on Film

Brimstone and Treacle
(1982) 85m R
Sting, Denholm Elliott
D: Richard Loncraine
Devilish houseguest ravishes host's comatose daughter, restores her! It's synchronicity!

Dogs in Space
(1987) 109m
Michael Hutchence, Saskia Post
D: Richard Lowenstein
Extreme burnouts hang in Melbourne circa 1978. Good gag involving Brian Eno record.

The Girl on a Motorcycle
(1968) 92m R
Marianne Faithful, Alain Delon
D: Jack Cardiff
Bored housewife joins major biker. They cruise, dwell on their sexual encounters.

The Man Who Fell to Earth
(1976) 118m R
David Bowie, Candy Clark
D: Nicolas Roeg
Alien assumes guise of peculiar earthling, becomes rich, but still can't get home. Ping-pong, anyone?

Ned Kelly
(1970) 100m PG
Mick Jagger
D: Tony Richardson
Australian wilderness is roamed by a pouty outlaw with massive lips.

Roadside Prophets
(1992) 96m R
John Doe, Adam Horovitz
D: Abbe Wool
X man and Beastie Boy bike cross country and encounter all manner of bizarre characters.

Trespass
(1992) 104 R
Ice T, Ice Cube
D: Walter Hill
Moronic firemen stumble into war between two crime lords. People get hurt.

Vibes
(1988) 99m PG
Cindy Lauper, Jeff Goldblum
D: Ken Kwapis
Wacky psychics find love and adventure in South America. You'll just want to have fun.

Who's That Girl?
(1987) 94m PG
Madonna, Griffin Dunne
D: James Foley
Wrongly convicted woman kidnaps her lawyer and searches for villain who framed her. Sort of a cross between *Bringing Up Baby* and the cover of Roxy Music's second album.

NEW YORK, NEW YORK
(1977) 163m PG
Liza Minnelli
D: Martin Scorsese

De Niro may have been more intense elsewhere, but it's doubtful that he's been more versatile. Here he's Jimmy Doyle, an obnoxious jazz saxophonist. WWII has just ended, and we first find him trying desperately to obtain temporary female companionship. His main target, a band singer, is initially repelled, but soon succumbs to his unlikely charm and humor. But then *her* career takes off, and the moody Doyle turns increasingly cruel. De Niro's characterization is at once repellant and fascinating, and his sax fingering is marvelous. Be warned, though: This is not a musical with a happy ending, or is it?

Some of Bob's Best:

A Bronx Tale (1993)

This Boy's Life (1993)

Night and the City (1992)

Backdraft (1991)

Cape Fear (1991)

Awakenings (1990)

Goodfellas (1990)

Jacknife (1989)

Midnight Run (1988)

The Untouchables (1987)

The Mission (1986)

Brazil (1985)

King of Comedy (1982)

True Confessions (1981)

Raging Bull (1980)

The Deer Hunter (1978)

Taxi Driver (1976)

The Godfather, Part 2 (1974)

Mean Streets (1973)

An American in Paris
(1951) 113m
Gene Kelly, Leslie Caron
D: Vincente Minnelli
Ex-GI remains in Paris after WW2 and falls for young woman who is, in turn, taken by older fellow. Features genre's single longest dance sequence.

Daddy Long Legs
(1955) 126m
Fred Astaire, Leslie Caron
D: Jean Negulesco
Eccentric millionaire becomes French orphan's anonymous benefactor. Her musings on his identity prompt some of the genre's most original, if inexplicable, dance sequences.

Dancers
(1987) 99m PG
Mikhail Baryshnikov, Julie Kent
D: Herbert Ross
Ballet-lover's extravaganza, featuring extensive portions of Giselle. But forget the parallel storyline, the performers already have.

Flashdance
(1983) 95m R
Jennifer Beals, Michael Nouri
D: Adrian Lyne
Welder by day, evocative dancer-choreographer by night. Fetching heroine finds love and success in the bar least likely to actually be found in Pittsburgh.

Footloose
(1984) 107m PG
Kevin Bacon, Lori Singer
D: Herbert Ross
Groovy kid incites teen peers into having fun in town ruled by oppressive minister. Nifty rafters-scooting scene.

Invitation to the Dance
(1956) 93m
Gene Kelly, Tamara Toumanova
D: Gene Kelly
Lesser-known work features 3 extended dance scenes. Those who love dance will love this one.

Saturday Night Fever
(1977) 118m R
John Travolta, Karen Gorney
D: John Badham
Brooklyn grunt tries to parlay disco-dance capabilities into success and thus obtain love of somewhat prim partner. Put on your white suit and start flicking the light switch.

Strictly Ballroom
(1992) 94m PG
Paul Mercurio, Tara Morice
D: Baz Luhrmann
Innovative dance contestant insists on doing things his own way. Endearing, good-natured fare with cult potential.

The Turning Point
(1977) 119m PG
Leslie Browne, Mikhail Baryshnikov
D: Herbert Ross
Forget the catfighting between leads Shirley MacLaine and Anne Bancroft, this one works best when it focuses on its talented, attractive, young ballet stars.

SWING TIME
(1936) 103m
Ginger Rogers
D: George Stevens

Astaire has never been more debonair and delightful than in this lighter-than-air comedy about a gambling-addict dancer who's already engaged when he meets the woman of his dreams. Fine pairing with Rogers. Tunes include: *The Way You Look Tonight, Never Gonna Dance, Pick Yourself Up, A Fine Romance,* and *Bojangles of Harlem*. Astaire's effortless tenor is, as always, a pleasure as well.

Putting on the Top Hat:

Top Hat (1935)

Follow the Fleet (1936)

Shall We Dance (1937)

Carefree (1938)

You'll Never Get Rich (1941)

Easter Parade (1948)

Let's Dance (1950)

Royal Wedding (1951)

Daddy Long Legs (1955)

Silk Stockings (1957)

And the nominees are:

A Christmas Carol
(1938) 70m
Reginald Owen, Gene Lockhart
D: Edwin L. Marin
Dickens classic well rendered, with particularly ominous graveyard scene. "God bless Tiny Tim."

Christmas in Connecticut
(1945) 101m
Barbara Stanwyck, Reginald Gardiner
D: Peter Godfrey
Prominent columnist on housekeeping risks exposure when publicity gimmick forces her to host war veteran for holidays. Avoid the remake.

A Christmas Story
(1983) 95m PG
Peter Billingsley, Darren McGavin
D: Bob Clark
Comedy about boy's single-minded obsession with obtaining a Red Ryder BB-gun for Christmas.

Fanny and Alexander
(1983) 197m R
Ewa Froling, Gunn Walgren
D: Ingmar Bergman
Extended family of stage folk wallow in yuletide reveling. That's the first hour. Next two include a classic battle between good and evil, with a despicable minister embodying the latter. Bergman at his brightest.

Holiday Inn
(1942) 101m
Fred Astaire, Bing Crosby
D: Mark Sandrich
Song-and-dance duo transform farm into inn open only during holidays. Remade as *White Christmas*. This one's better.

It's a Wonderful Life
(1946) 125m
James Stewart, Donna Reed
D: Frank Capra
Suicidal hero gets glimpse of alternative events courtesy of bumbling angel. Jeepers, it must be Christmas again.

Miracle on 34th Street
(1947) 97m
Edmund Gween, Maureen O'Hara
D: George Seaton
Macy's Santa insists he's the real Kris Kringle and must prove his claims (and sanity) to the courts and a skeptical young girl (Natalie Wood). Just think, it's the U.S. Post Office that saves the day.

National Lampoon's Christmas Vacation
(1989) 93m PG-13
Chevy Chase, Beverly D'Angelo
D: Jeremiah S. Chechik
Moronic father and hapless family host squadron of ignorant, repellent relatives. May hit too close to home for some viewers.

White Christmas
(1954) 120m
Bing Crosby, Danny Kaye
D: Michael Curtiz
Remake of *Holiday Inn* concerns comedy duo who transform farm into inn to raise money for charity. Catch the original instead, knock back an egg nog, and drive yourself nuts waiting in vain for Kaye.

And the winner is:

Santa Claus Conquers the Martians

(1964) 80m

John Call, Pia Zadora

D: Nicholas Webster

The title says it all! Zadora's just a tyke in this one, which means she looks like herself anyway.

The Birth of a Nation
(1915) 175m
Lillian Gish, Mae Marsh
D: *D.W. Griffith*
Epic saga about America. With pro-KKK sentiments, this is hardly a PC pic. Better remembered for its technical leaps.

Broken Blossoms
(1919) 102m
Lillian Gish, Richard Barthelmess
D: *D.W. Griffith*
Pitiful waif, brutalized by dad, is befriended by Chinaman in London's squalid Limehouse district.

Intolerance
(1916) 175m
Lillian Gish, Mae Marsh
D: *D.W. Griffith*
Ambitious, multi-narrative epic about intolerance through the ages. As unappealing as it sounds, but the sets are quite impressive.

Metropolis
(1926) 115m
Brigitte Helm, Alfred Abel
D: *Fritz Lang*
Fetching, flirtatious robot nearly drives workers to rebel in bleak future of fat cats and laborers. One of Adolf Hitler's favorites.

Napoleon
(1927) 235m
Albert Dieudonne, Antonin Artaud
D: *Abel Gance*
Ambitious epic replete with dizzying camerawork and extraordinary triple-screen imagery.

Pandora's Box
(1928) 110m
Louise Brooks, Francis Lederer
D: *G.W. Pabst*
Classic marking the end of the German Expressionist era finds Brooks as the tempestuous Lulu, who destroys everyone around her and meets her fate at the hands of Jack the Ripper. See also the second Brooks/Pabst collaboration *Diary of a Lost Girl* (1929).

Un Chien Andalou
(1928) 20m
Pierre Batcheff, Simone Marevil
D: *Luis Bunuel, Salvador Dali*
Surrealist classic replete with ants emerging from a hole in the hero's hand. This one's just the right length for repeated viewings. Keep an eye out for it.

Way Down East
(1920) 107m
Lillian Gish, Richard Barthelmess
D: *D.W. Griffith*
Gish drifts on an ice flow in this classic melodrama. (Meaning: There's one good scene in this one, and everyone overacts.)

A Woman of Paris
(1923) 111m
Edna Purviance, Adolphe Menjou
D: *Charlie Chaplin*
Poignant drama about a kept woman. Strong performance from Purviance. Chaplin appears briefly as a porter.

The Birds
(1963) 120m
Rod Taylor, Tippi Hedren
D: Alfred Hitchcock
Vicious birds unite and turn on Bodega Bay community. Answer: A venal wren. Question: How did Taylor get his cleft chin?

Dressed to Kill
(1980) 105 R
Keith Gordon, Angie Dickinson, Nancy Allen, Michael Caine
D: Brian DePalma
Enterprising young man tries to solve mother's murder, gets help from gorgeous prostitute, who's being stalked by really ugly woman.

Dune
(1984) 137m PG-13
Kyle MacLachlan, Sean Young
D: David Lynch
Absolute masterpiece of Huh? cinema. Whole scenes, whole storylines go absolutely nowhere. And the big deal is some giant worms that look like outtakes from American Sportsman as directed by Ed Wood. Incredible in every negative way.

The Fury
(1978) 117m R
Kirk Douglas, Andrew Stevens
D: Brian DePalma
You gotta like any movie in which a levitating villain can fall off a roof. There's also a terrorist attack that's actually designed to kidnap Stevens. Haven't he seen *Night Eyes*?

Jacob's Ladder
(1990) 116m R
Tim Robbins, Elizabeth Pena
D: Adrian Lyne
Whole lot of odd things are happening to psychotic Vietnam vet. Robbins manages to be smug even when he's bewildered. The ending will make you feel really stupid and angry.

True Stories
(1986) 89m PG
David Byrne, John Goodman
D: David Byrne
Celebrate with the eccentric denizens of an off-center Texas town, including the Laziest Woman in America (Swoosie Kurtz).

Twin Peaks: Fire Walk with Me
(1992) 135m R
Sheryl Lee, Kyle MacLachlan
D: David Lynch
Utterly inexplicable film about holy slut who's doomed to horrible demise. Lynch's most characteristic film.

Videodrome
(1983) 87m
James Woods, Deborah Harry
D: David Cronenberg
Channel surfer finds S&M show featuring vocalist from Blondie! She puts a pin through her nipple, then disappears as the hero begins experiencing some grotesque physical changes.

And the nominees are:

Bambi
(1942) 69m G
D: David Hand
Fawn learns that life in the forest is
not all fun and games. Mom's death
gets parents everytime.

Barfly
(1987) 100m R
Mickey Rourke, Faye Dunaway
D: Barbet Schroeder
Filthy, obnoxious writer wallows in
alcohol-induced haze. Rourke superb in tailored role.

Baxter
(1991) 82m
*Francois Driancourt, Lise
   Delamare*
D: Jerome Boivin
Comedy about dog's experiences in
various households. From the dog's
perspective.

Beethoven
(1992) 89m PG
Charles Grodin, Bonnie Hunt
D: Brian Levant
St. Bernard puppy wanders into
home, endears himself to occupants. Meanwhile, evil doctors want
the pooch for experiments. Oh, da
joy. Followed by more puppies in
Beethoven's 2nd.

Benji
(1974) 87m G
Peter Breck, Christopher Connelly
D: Joe Camp
Dog falls in love, rescues children.
Box office hit sired multiple sugary
sequels.

Black Beauty
(1946) 74m
Mona Freeman, Richard Denning
D: Max Nosseck
Young girl develops affection for
amazing horse. You'll develop a
headache.

Black Cat
(1981) 92m
Patrick Magee, Mimsy Farmer
D: Lucio Fulci
Deranged medium summons dead,
places their spirits in his pet cat.
Yeah, but does he throw the cat in
the river?

Black Stallion
(1979) 120m PG
Kelly Reno, Mickey Rooney
D: Carroll Ballard
Boy bonds with horse after they're
shipwrecked together. When they
return to civilization, things get
racy.

Lassie
(1994) 92m PG
Helen Slater, Jon Tenney
D: Daniel Petrie
Umpteenth film starring everyone's favorite collie who, once again, comes to the rescue of her none-too-bright family.

White Fang
(1991) 109m PG
Ethan Hawke, Klaus Maria Brandauer
D: Randal Kleiser
Jack London adventure tale finds boy befriending heroic canine during Alaskan gold rush.

And the winner is:

Bringing Up Baby

(1938) 103m

Cary Grant, Katharine Hepburn

D: Howard Hawks

Screwball comedy about dinosaur-bones specialist who falls in with socialite and her leopard. There's also a truly remarkable dog, George.

Title Index

127